HAYDN
THE INNOVATOR

HAYDN
THE INNOVATOR

A New Approach to the
String Quartets

Edited by
David Young

with an introduction by
H.C. Robbins Landon

RNCM
ROYAL NORTHERN
COLLEGE OF MUSIC

in association with

2000

Published by Arc Music
Nanholme Mill, Shaw Wood Road
Todmorden, Lancs. OL14 6DA

Design by Tony Ward
Printed at the Arc & Throstle Press
Nanholme Mill, Todmorden, Lancs.

ISBN 1 900072 37 8

ACKNOWLEDGEMENTS
The musical examples throughout the text are re-
produced by kind permission of Alfred A. Kalmus
Ltd., London.

The publishers wish to thank the Principal, staff and
students of the Royal Northern College of Music
for the provision of the CD accompanying this book.
Particular thanks are due to Christopher Rowland,
Director of Chamber Music at the RNCM and Artistic Director of the RNCM's HaydnFest in 1999;
Baz Barker, Recording Manager at the RNCM; John
Egan, Assistant Recording Manager at the RNCM;
and the members of the Yeomans String Quartet.

The essays by Michael Spitzer and David Young appeared in summary form in the *Journal of the Haydn
Society of Great Britain*, No. 19, 1999.

Contents

Editor's Preface / 7
    David Young

Introduction / 9
    H.C. Robbins Landon

Reading Haydn's Quartets / 11
    John Irving

The First Movements / 33
    Denis McCaldin

The Slow Movements / 57
    David Young

Minuets and Trios in Haydn's Quartets / 81
    David Wyn Jones

Haydn's Quartet Finales and Cyclical Closure / 99
    Michael Spitzer

Performing Haydn's Quartets / 121
    Alan George

Appendices
    Chronological List of Haydn's String Quartets / 137
    List of Printed Musical Examples / 141
    About the Authors and Performers / 145
    Select Bibliography / 149
    Index / 151

Editor's Preface

This book originated in a remarkable festival held at the Royal Northern College of Music between Friday 8 January and Sunday 10 January 1999, during which all of Haydn's string quartets were performed. During this 'HaydnFest', as it was called, leading professional, amateur, and student string quartets joined together with musicologists, instrument makers, book and music sellers and general music lovers for a glorious celebration of Haydn's quartets. Apart from the continuous performances, there were masterclasses, lessons, a 'Haydnseek' for children, exhibitions and four 'seminars' under the general title of 'Haydn the Innovator'.

Expanded versions of these seminars – by Denis McCaldin on the first movements, David Young on the slow movements, David Wyn Jones on the minuet and trio movements, and Michael Spitzer on the finales – form chapters II-V of this book. Additional framing chapters have been provided by John Irving, who places the quartets as a whole in historical context, and Alan George, who discusses performance issues from the perspective of an experienced viola player with a leading quartet.

The subtitle of the book – *A New Approach to the String Quartets* – is perhaps justified by the way in which the central chapters are organised around movement types, as opposed to the more conventional arrangement in chronological groups – such as the early, Eszterháza, Tost, London and post-London quartets. By adopting the present approach, each movement type is given full consideration, thereby avoiding the traditional analytical emphasis on first movements, so that the reader is able to appreciate fully how Haydn's invention extends equally to all four or – in the case of opp. 1 and 2 – five movements.

The accompanying CD consists of twenty-two examples, continuously numbered throughout the book, and mainly in the form of complete movements which are cross-referenced from the text; for example '[CD 10]' refers to the tenth track of the CD (which happens to be the slow movement of op. 64 no. 5). All the examples are performed by the Yeomans String Quartet, a recent student quartet of the Royal Northern College of Music which played a prominent part in the HaydnFest.

All the musical examples are taken from the Doblinger edition of the complete quartets, edited by Reginald Barrett Ayres and H.C. Robbins Landon, the only complete *Urtext* edition currently available. In many cases the examples are complete and so further reference to the scores will be unnecessary. In other cases, however, particularly in connection with Chapters I and VI, reference to the scores may be necessary for a full appreciation of the discussion. We are most grateful to Alfred A. Kalmus Ltd (on behalf of Doblinger K.G.) for permission to reproduce such a large number of musical examples.

It is a pleasure to record our thanks to Rosemary Williamson, Librarian of the Royal Northern College of Music, for procuring scores and parts, and to David Ledbetter for assistance in compiling the list of Haydn's quartets. Grateful thanks also are due to Christopher Rowland, Director of Chamber Music at the Royal Northern College of Music, Artistic Director of the HaydnFest, and the source of inspiration for this book. And finally to H.C. Robbins Landon, who has perhaps done more than anyone else to reveal the full glory of Haydn's legacy, and who has graced our work with an introduction.

David Young
December 2000

Introduction

H.C. Robbins Landon

It was a courageous and, in the end, highly successful idea to play all Haydn's string quartets in one weekend at Manchester. We need to be exposed to Haydn's music, which risks losing its message if it is only 'studied' rather than played. Even a generation after Haydn's death, his message was being misunderstood. Consider the following letter from Fanny Hensel, Felix Mendelssohn-Bartholdy's sister, to Beethoven's pupil, Felix Moscheles, on the subject of Haydn's quartet op. 76 no. 5 with its famous slow movement:

> Do you still remember, dear Herr Moscheles, that one evening during the autumn that he spent with us Felix played the wonderful Adagio in F sharp major from a Haydn Quartet? Father loved Haydn especially, every piece was new for him and moved him strangely. He wept when he heard it and said afterwards that he found it so profoundly sad. This description astonished Felix greatly, because *Mesto* [sadly] was in the tempo and all the rest of us in fact found that it rather made an impression of cheerfulness on us...[1]

Here, surely, is the crux of the matter: it is not the first time, nor will it be the last, that we observe the language of a composer gradually ceasing to carry its message to the audiences. That which was obviously profoundly sad to Haydn and his contemporary audiences was no longer sad but on the contrary jolly (*heiter*) to the young Mendelssohns, and probably to most young people. Of course this mental block about the eighteenth century was not limited to Haydn but also extended to Mozart, and in some respects the many nineteenth-century and even twentieth-century misunderstandings of such works as *Così fan tutte* are more incomprehensible than the general lack of respect for Haydn. When Cobbett's *Cyclopaedia of Chamber Music* appeared with an article on Mozart by Abert, the editor felt constrained – and this was the 1920s! – to warn his readers that Abert's concept of Mozart, with its demonic side, would be very new and strange

---

[1] Carl Ferdinand Pohl, *Joseph Haydn*, III (Leipzig: Hugo Botstiber, 1927), p. 313.

to most Anglo-Saxon lovers of that composer. The above extract from an account of a soirée at the Mendelssohns' house in Berlin is prophetic of what was to come and shows in a dramatic fashion the 'generation gap' in an appreciation of Haydn's music.

This curious gap still persists. In the Proms, Cecilia Bartoli gave a concert of Haydn and Mozart, conducted by Nikolaus Harnoncourt, including Haydn's dramatic *Scena di Berenice* (London, 1795), which has been often compared to Beethoven's *Ah! perfido!* of 1796. But in a review in the *Guardian Weekly* (29 July - 4 August 1999), this extraordinary work – Haydn's finest piece of music for dramatic soprano – is described as '... essentially rather dull and lifeless'. The *Scena*'s message was simply not understood.

That is why the 'Quartet Marathon' served a highly useful function. Listen, and observe carefully what Haydn is trying to say.

I

Reading Haydn's Quartets

John Irving

INTRODUCTION

The following, purely coincidental circumstance led [Haydn] to try his hand at the composition of quartets. A Baron Fürnberg had an estate in Weinzierl, several stages from Vienna; and from time to time he invited his parish priest, his estates' manager, Haydn and Albrechtsberger (a brother of the well-known contrapuntist who played the violoncello) in order to have a little music. Fürnberg asked Haydn to write something that could be played by these four friends of the Art. Haydn, who was then eighteen years old, accepted the proposal, and so originated his first Quartet.[1]

In this much-cited anecdote, recorded by Haydn's biographer, Georg August Griesinger, Haydn recalls at the end of his life the origin of the string quartet as an almost accidental occurrence to provide pleasing domestic diversion. It is a commonplace of the Haydn literature. And yet, as with all anecdotes, its context is as powerful as its content. In such cases, how we read the story is as important as what we read. So, how are we to read this one? By virtue of its situation within an authorised biographical record, it acquires a certain authority. By virtue of its date, moreover, it acquires a certain potency in relation to public perception of Haydn's music.

The composer invites us to view those earliest productions in the light of his subsequent transformation and development of the genre over almost half a century.[2] By the early nineteenth century, when Haydn's discussions with his biographer took place, he had raised the string quartet to a level commensurate

[1] 'Biographische Notizen über Joseph Haydn', serialised in *Allgemeine musikalische Zeitung* xi (1809), pp. 641, 657, 673, 689, 705, 721, 737, 776 and issued in Leipzig the following year as a single work. This English translation is from H.C. Robbins Landon, *Haydn: Chronicle and Works: The Early Years* (London: Thames & Hudson, 1976), p. 228.
[2] Probably Haydn's memory was a little suspect here: if these first quartets were really composed at the age of 18, then they must date from around 1750. No quartets earlier than opp. 1 and 2 are known. They first appeared in print between 1764 and 1766, and it is now generally accepted that the works referred to in Griesinger's account actually date from about 1757.

with that of the sonata, symphony and concerto – 'public' genres disseminated across a wide geographical area, and within
which composers' reputations were gained or lost. The shifting
status of the quartet in Haydn's hands led to important developments in style. The opp. 71 and 74 sets, written for Count
Apponyi in 1793 and published respectively in 1795 and 1796,
were specifically designed for professional performance.[3] László
Somfai has noted that these works contrast in several important
respects with Haydn's earlier quartet sets, notably in their adop-
tion of gestures more typically encountered in his later symphonies, and perhaps specifically aimed at the expectations of London audiences.[4] Features such as the slow introduction to op. 71
no. 2, and the tendency towards an initial *forte* chordal flourish
– for instance, in op. 71 no. 1 (actually a *closing* gesture), or the
more extended introduction to op. 74 no. 3, whose imperfect
cadential close on the dominant (*forte*) is separated from the 'true'
beginning (*piano*) by eight beats of silence[5] – are quite rare in
Haydn's earlier quartets and imply that their communicative
process involves an essential measure of interaction with an audience. It seems that these quartets are purposely designed to be
listened to from without as well as from within (by the players
themselves); that is, the audience is a vital ingredient in their
representation. Mary Hunter has recently argued that virtuosic
episodes in these pieces also acquire a dimension of meaning specifically from the concert situation (one thinks of such movements as the finale of op. 71 no. 3):

> Virtuosic or 'brilliant' passages may reveal that the composer
> has clearly constructed a moment in which the audience's atten-
> tion is meant to be directed to the performer's capacity to repro-
> duce the difficult passagework he has written.[6]

[3] They were presented by the Salomon Quartet in Johann Peter Salomon's 1794
concert series, during Haydn's second London visit.
[4] 'Haydn's London String Quartets', in *Haydn Studies: Proceedings of the
International Haydn Conference, Washington D.C. 1975*, ed. Jens Peter Larsen,
Howard Serwer and James Webster (New York: Norton, 1981), pp. 389-91.
[5] Note also the breach in textural continuity here: unison (later chordal)
introduction, followed by polyphony.
[6] 'Haydn's London Piano Trios and His Salomon String Quartets: Private vs.
Public?', in *Haydn and His World* ed. Elaine Sisman (Princeton: Princeton
University Press, 1997), pp. 103-30 (at p. 110).

Such a mode of utterance is a far cry from those humble beginnings at the Fürnberg estate. Haydn left the quartet in a wholly different state from that in which he found(ed) it. He had made the quartet genre his own in a period which Carl Dahlhaus identifies with an emerging conception of music as an arena in which the composer's personal sentiment (expressed, for instance in the idiom of *Empfindsamkeit* ['expansive' or 'sentimental style'] so strongly projected in the F minor quartet, op. 20 no. 5) might be located.[7] While Haydn did not actually invent the string quartet, his extensive contribution to the genre, continually experimenting with ways in which the particular instrumental combination and the musical material might be brought into an ideal synthesis, he, more than any of his contemporaries, established its 'serious' credentials. In doing so, Haydn was able to exploit his pan-European status as the most respected composer of the late eighteenth century.

Haydn created a repertoire of quartets. From our retrospective stance, we are entitled to approach that repertoire as a 'totality' in need of explanation. The identity of that totality will depend on the approach taken, of course; one that focuses on the quartets in a structuralist way will describe a totality different from that emerging out of a study of their reception (even if we understand a structuralist approach to be simply one facet of the reception-history of classic period instrumental music).

In the first case, that which is studied resides in the music itself, and is assumed to embody authorial intention. In the second, the object of study is located in the response of the reader/performer/listener and is an acknowledgement that the musical text is not fixed, but flexible, its intention not authorial (or, at least, not wholly so) but subtly nuanced according to the changing intellectual agendas and cultural environments of the work's audiences – dimensions of the work that the composer could not aspire to control.

In what follows, the repertoire is explored insofar as its identity is revealed in discourses of various kinds, navigating between contemporary (that is, eighteenth-century) and modern critiques and between internal and external frames of reference for Haydn's quartets. These include Haydn's relations with his publish-

---

[7] *Foundations of Music History* translated by J. Bradford Robinson (Cambridge: Cambridge University Press, 1983), pp. 21-2.

ers; early critical responses; compositional imperatives, specifically the provision of aesthetic 'balance' between the individual
characters and compositional features of the four movements;
the notion of an intertextual identity for this repertoire; and a
critique of the very notion of the 'holistic' quartet comprised
of four interlocking and complementary movements, focusing
especially on the question of whether the overarching connections habitually observed by commentators on this repertoire
are truly essences located in the music itself, or are simply mental constructs residing in our own approaches to Haydn's quartets, inevitably inflected by the consideration of philosophies
of musical unity deriving from the study of later (especially
nineteenth-century symphonic) repertoires.

THE CONCEPT OF REPERTOIRE

We need to begin with the important caveat that this 'repertoire' is partly retrospective fiction. It was not, from the viewpoint of Haydn and his contemporaries, a 'project' to invent
the quartet by providing it with a substantial repertoire over
the course of nearly fifty years (though that is, in fact, what
happened). For the composer, the circumstances were generally
pragmatic, the earliest efforts, recollected in the quotation above,
fulfilling a desire for occasional music to play in private. Subsequent quartets were responses of differing kinds, sometimes em-
bodying the composer's own wish to experiment with technical or textural problems, such as fugal writing in three of the
op. 20 finales, or else the situation of virtuosity within a
concertante framework, as in the op. 17 quartets, or in opp. 54,
55 and 64. Yet others were the result of particular commissions.
It is important to remember in the following pages that Haydn's quartets retain multiple identities, and that the idea of continual progression towards an ideal form throughout opp. 9,
17, 20, 33, 42, 50, 54, 55, 64, 71, 74, 76 and 77 is not an inherent
process, but a mental construction.[8] The later quartets do not
exercise a monopoly of 'greatness' in Haydn's quartet production.

Publication was a key element in building the quartet reper-

---

[8] This series reflects Haydn's own view that his mature quartet writing began
only with op. 9, and leaves out of consideration the incomplete quartet op. 103.

toire. Haydn's quartets were widely disseminated in print, frequently by more than one publisher, in Vienna, Paris, Berlin, Amsterdam, London and elsewhere. Typically, they appeared in groups of six works, in which Haydn aimed to provide a varied profile, within which each quartet stood out for its individuality rather than its conformity to a stereotype. Publishers were keen to alert potential purchasers to the appearance of new collections of Haydn's quartets, regularly placing announcements in the press either of brand new works, or else of reissues, the latter practice underlining an important, and rather novel dimension of Haydn's quartets, their longevity.

The Viennese firm, Artaria, placed an advertisement in the *Wiener Zeitung*, 3 May 1800, for a re-issue of the op. 20 quartets, *Edition Revue et Corrigée... par l'Auteur*: "diese Auflage ist nun die erste und einzige welche in ihrer ganzen Ächtheit da das Werk aus der Hand des Verfassers selbst kommt, da ist." ["... the only wholly genuine edition of the work in existence, stemming directly from the hand of the composer."][9] By this date, op. 20 had been in circulation for nearly thirty years, a remarkable degree of permanence, suggestive of a significant shift of emphasis in the contemporary perception of instrumental music according to which these quartets were perceived as works of profound artistic content, worthy to be revisited again and again, and valuable in an enduring aesthetic sense which sets them somewhat apart from the merely local, immediate and functional status typically accorded to chamber music at this time. Notice that in Artaria's announcement, a distinction is made between 'diese Auflage' and 'das Werk'. The 'work' was now something lying behind the notes that could only be *represented* in a text; something that might, indeed, be corrupted by widespread and perhaps indiscriminate circulation, but whose essential 'truth' endured nevertheless and was here represented in Artaria's newly revised edition proceeding directly from the composer. By implication, Haydn's quartets were to be regarded by the purchaser as serious artistic statements, to which a dimension of 'authenticity' ('Ächtheit') might be imputed.

Thus objectified, Haydn's quartets also acquired, through the medium of print, a commercial status, and in this respect, the

---

[9] Anthony van Hoboken, *Joseph Haydn: Thematisch-Bibliographisches Werkverzeichnis* Band I (Mainz: Schott, 1957), p. 391.

composer was just as much an innovator as in the purely compositional sphere. Incidentally, Haydn's correspondence with his publishers provides an illuminating insight into his developing perception of the quartet genre. It becomes clear that he viewed his quartets increasingly as public representations, rather than trifles intended for domestic entertainment. What also emerges from the correspondence is that Haydn regarded these pieces as vehicles through which to manipulate his publishers in order to secure the maximum financial return.

As is well-known, Haydn pre-empted the publication of his op. 33 quartets by Artaria in 1782 by offering 'correctly-copied' manuscripts of these new quartets on private subscription. He evidently had a number of near-identical letters of invitation prepared, which he then signed and dispatched to selected persons of note. Only three of these letters are known to survive, the first to the physiologist, Johann Caspar Lavater of Zürich, the second to Fürsten Kraft Ernst zu Öttingen-Wallerstein, and the third to Abbot Robert Schlecht of Salmannsweiler (Baden). All are dated 3 December 1781, and include the tempting comment that these quartets, the first he had composed for a decade, were written 'in an entirely new and special way'.[10] It is not known how many recipients rose to this bait, but any who did so would have been unaware that, by this stage, Haydn had already sold the same works to the publisher Artaria.[11] Shortly afterwards, the composer became alarmed at Artaria's announcement in the *Wiener Zeitung* (29 December 1781) that op. 33 would be published the following month, since he had hoped to secure a reasonable financial return from his private subscribers before the works appeared on general sale.[12]

In the case of the op. 50 quartets, Haydn's duplicity reached new heights. He offered these works to the English publisher,

---

[10] The text is slightly different in each letter. That to Lavater reads: "sie sind von einer Neu, gantz besonderer Art"; that to Öttingen-Wallerstein, "sie sind auf eine gantz neue besondere Art". Haydn's letters to Lavater and Öttingen-Wallerstein are published in *Joseph Haydn Gesammelte Briefe und Aufzeichnungen: Unter Benützung der Quellensammlung von H.C. Robbins Landon*. (Kassel: Bärenreiter, 1965), nos. 39, 40. (Henceforth *Briefe*, from which all quotations in this section are taken.) That to Schlecht is reprinted in Georg Feder, 'Ein vergessener Haydn-Brief' in *Haydn-Studien* I/2 (1966), p. 115.

[11] *Briefe* no. 38a, 18 October 1781.

[12] *Briefe* no. 41, 4 January 1782.

William Forster, along with the 'Paris' symphonies for 25 guineas in a letter dated 8 August 1787,[13] assuring him that these were works "qui ne sont pas sortie de ma main". It would seem from a second letter to Forster the following month that Haydn had entered into a formal contract with this publisher,[14] a circumstance which caused him considerable difficulty in his relations with Artaria, to whom he had also sold op. 50, since Artaria was informed by their English agents of the appearance of Forster's English edition.[15]

Undaunted by this close shave, Haydn continued his dubious marketing strategy in future quartets. On 15 August 1799, he expressed his concern that Artaria was about to publish the op. 76 quartets, thus pre-empting the English edition to be issued by Longman and Broderip, with whom the composer had previously concluded a deal valid for five years whereby that firm had 'exclusive' rights to Haydn's 'new' works.[16] Once again, Haydn was in trouble because of his shady tactics; if the London firm had discovered that Artaria had already acquired the same quartets directly from the composer, he would have been in

---

[13] *Briefe*, no. 95.

[14] *Briefe*, no. 97, 20 September 1787.

[15] Haydn's initial excuse was that a copyist in Artaria's workshop must have made duplicates which he had sold to the English firm; he then shifted his ground somewhat, acknowledging that he had sent one of the op. 50 quartets to Forster himself (but only after Artaria had engraved them). Both claims are manifestly false. For Haydn's letters to Artaria, see *Briefe*, nos. 98, 7 October 1787 and 100, 27 September 1787; the subject is discussed in detail in W. Dean Sutcliffe, *Haydn String Quartets Op. 50* (Cambridge: Cambridge University Press, 1992), pp. 33-6. In a further letter to Forster of 28 February 1788 (*Briefe*, no. 105), Haydn names his price for 'exclusive' publication rights to his future compositions: "wer von mir 6 neue Stücke für sich allein besitzen will, mehr als 20 guiné spendiren muß. Ich hab in der that unlängst mit Jemand einen Contract geschlossen, so mir für jedesmahlige 6 Stücke 100, und mehr guinéen bezahlt." ["Whoever wants exclusive rights to 6 new pieces of mine must pay more than 20 guineas. In fact, I have recently concluded a contract with someone whereby I am paid 100 guineas and more for each 6 pieces."]

[16] *Briefe*, no. 231.

breach of contract to the tune of £75 sterling.[17] Op. 76 was issued in two sets of three quartets. The first appeared in London five weeks before Artaria's Viennese print; the second, however, appeared in Vienna on 7 December 1799, but in London only on 25 April 1800.[18]

What emerges strongly from all this is a sense of Haydn's supreme confidence in the artistic worth of his quartets. He evidently felt that these pieces merited a more than decent financial return, and in order to secure one, he was prepared to resort to double-dealing, possibly because there were, as yet, no established commercial structures in place to ensure that a composer such as Haydn received adequate support in the free market. This is an important factor, since it was in part through the medium of the string quartet that Haydn stepped outside the conventional boundaries imposed by princely patronage. His quartets gradually acquired a cultural status, one that reconfigured them as objects of aesthetic enquiry rather than mere *Gebrauchmusik*. This transformation is noticeable, too, in critical responses to the published quartets.

Two common themes running through reviews of Haydn's published quartets that appeared in German periodical literature during the last quarter of the eighteenth century are the acknowledgement of Haydn's pre-eminence (a role that the quartets helped him to secure), and the association between the use of remote, sometimes chromatic melody or harmony and *genius*, a category that emerges strongly in aesthetics at this time and which marks a realignment of cultural values in art, moving away from the dominant Aristotelian concept of *mimesis* towards a neo-Platonic

---

[17] In fact, the London edition had probably already appeared by the date of Haydn's letter to Artaria (15 August 1799). Charles Burney wrote to the composer on 19 August 1799, remarking that "I had the great pleasure of hearing your new quartetti (opera 76) well performed... and never received more pleasure from instrumental music; they are full of invention, fire, good taste, and new effects, and seem the production, not of a sublime genius who has written so much and so well already, but of one of highly-cultivated talents, who had expended none of his fire before... La cadenza [to the variations on the 'Emperor's Hymn' in op. 76 no. 3] particolarmente mi pare nuova e squisitissima." ["... the cadenza appears to me to be especially novel and exquisite."] *Briefe*, no. 232.

[18] Haydn had originally written these six quartets in response to a commission from Count Erdödy for which he received a fee of 100 ducats; see *Briefe*, pp. 334.

view privileging intuition, and stressing the individual personality of the artist.[19]

A Balanced View: The Four-Movement Design

Having departed from the five-movement arch-like structure of opp. 1 and 2, in which not only the presence of two minuets, but also the textures (involving extended stretches of simple theme and chordal accompaniment, or else unison and/or octave doubling) are suggestive of a close connection with the world of the divertimento,[20] Haydn faced the important challenge of replacing a ready-made satisfying symmetrical balance of fast-minuet-slow-minuet-fast, within the frame of just four movements. If we were to attempt a history of Haydn's quartets from op. 9 onwards, one way of arranging the narrative would

---

[19] Space forbids further consideration of this crucial aesthetic shift that was to prefigure the romantic movement. Aristotle's philosophy of art is outlined specifically in the *Poetics*, a book whose centrality to literary criticism extended well into the eighteenth century. It was the foundation of Charles Batteux's *Les Beaux-Arts réduits à une Même Principe* (Paris, 1746, and many later editions). Batteux's treatise, which focuses on the principle of *mimesis* in the arts, was translated by Johann Christoph Gottsched as *Auszug aus des Herrn Batteux schönen Künsten aus dem einzigen Grundsätze der Nachahmung hergeleitet* (Leipzig, 1754). For an English translation of Aristotle's *Poetics*, see D.A. Russell & M. Winterbottom (eds.), *Classical Literary Criticism* (Oxford: Oxford University Press, 1972; rev. 1989), pp. 51-90. The neo-Platonic aesthetic derives from texts such as Plato's *Phaedrus* and *Ion*, which deal with types of 'divine madness' by which the artist is, from time to time, possessed and which allowed him to give voice to the spiritual in art, and also from the writings of Longinus, whose *De Sublimate* (*On the Sublime*) had become one of the most widely known of ancient classical texts since its translation into French by Nicolas Boileau in 1674. For English translations, see *Phaedrus and Letters VII and VIII* transl. W. Hamilton (Harmondsworth and London: Penguin, 1973) and *Classical Literary Criticism* (Oxford: Oxford University Press, 1989). On this general issue see the seminal text by Joel. S. Springarn, 'The Origins of Modern Criticism' in *Modern Philology* vol. 1 / 4 (1904), pp. 326-8. Also, Milton C. Nahm, *Readings in Philosophy of Art and Aesthetics* (Englewood Cliffs, N. J: Prentice Hall, 1975), Bellamy Hosler, *Changing Aesthetic Views of Instrumental Music in Eighteenth-Century Germany* (Ann Arbor: UMI Press, 1981) and John Neubauer, *The Emancipation of Music from Language: Departure from Mimesis in Eighteenth-Century Aesthetics* (New Haven: Yale University Press, 1986). For a selection of these reviews, see Mary Sue Morrow, *German Music Criticism in the Late Eighteenth Century* (Cambridge: Cambridge University Press, 1997), pp. 61, 64, 111, and H.C. Robbins Landon, *Haydn Chronicle and Works: Haydn at Eszterháza 1766-1790* (London: Thames & Hudson, 1978), pp. 466-7, and *Haydn in England* (London: Thames & Hudson, 1976), p. 236

[20] Indeed, a *continuo* in-filling would not be inappropriate in some places.

be to chart the manifold ways in which he rose to that challenge, investing his four-movement quartets with the poise necessary to avoid a lopsided effect whereby one movement (usually the first, in sonata form) attains undue prominence, leaving the others as mere appendages.

His solutions to this problem are many and varied. One approach is to treat the four movements as an unfolding process, to which the finale provides a culmination, as for example in the fugal finales to op. 20, or that of op. 64 no. 5 ('The Lark'), whose ternary structure incorporates a substantial middle episode fugato in the tonic minor, providing a radical enough contrast to the opening *vivace* section to require this to be significantly expanded in length and in texture on its return (note especially the 'thickness' of semiquaver polyphony from b. 100 to the end, compared to bb. 1-28 – a feature obviously set in train by the experience of the preceding fugato and which produces a fitting sense of closure not just to the finale, but to the quartet as a whole). Another is to ensure adequate counterbalance between the various dimensions across the quartet as a whole: fast and slow tempi; dance-like and contrapuntal textures; *concertante* writing, or virtuoso display and integrated polyphony. Attention to detail such as this allows for the foregrounding of even quite extended passages or movements, provided that these are smoothed-out elsewhere in the design. For example, the peculiarly intense slow movement of op. 76 no. 4 ('The Sunrise') carries considerable weight within the work as a whole, but Haydn is careful not to allow it to overwhelm the other movements. It is preceded by a substantial first movement, in which both 'first' and 'second' subjects are subdivided into a number of discrete thematic parts, and treated to a fulsome development. When it eventually arrives, therefore, the slow movement settles into an already established pattern of spaciousness and does not seem at all out of place.

Another way in which Haydn avoids the impression of 'saturation' within just a single dimension is illustrated by the B minor quartet, op. 64 no. 2. One of the 'Tost' quartets, written for the former concertmaster of the Esterházy orchestra, it contains unusually virtuosic sections, obviously catering to the technical wizardry of Johann Tost. In order to escape the impression of just this one voice dominating the texture, Haydn sees to it that there are features other than virtuosity to capture the attention.

For example, in the first movement, there is the deliberate un-
certainty of tonality; it appears to begin in D, rather than the
tonic, B minor (eventually clarified at b. 5). The harmonic profile of the B major *Adagio* is richly-inflected by chromaticism,
situated within a variation structure and a carefully-crafted environment of tessitura, articulation and dynamic contrast that allows each instrument to shine. In the Minuet and Trio, emphasis is placed on opposite modality, the internal contrast of *stac-
cato-legato* being heightened by the introduction of a pronounced
Hungarian folk-idiom in the Minuet. In contrast to the polyphony that energises all three of these movements, the *Presto*
finale offers a high proportion of unison writing, injecting yet
another foil to the commanding presence of the first violin, and
ensuring that, as a whole, this quartet embraces a distinctive range
of characters.

A different strategy is offered by op. 50 no. 3 in E flat. Here,
the outer movements are monothematic sonata designs whose
development sections engage quite strongly in rigorous imitative counterpoint. That feature lends an overarching balance to
the work, to which the two inner movements provide a suitable
counterfoil. The expansive slow movement is a hybrid form,
embracing elements of variation, ternary and rondo.[21] The Minuet
and Trio are thematically interrelated, but hint at material from
the other movements, principally by virtue of the concentration on tonic and dominant pitches. So, while the outer movements apply a monothematic approach as balancing counterpoles
at either end of the quartet, they are separated by movements
that feature thematic variety as a *modus operandi*. The result is a
satisfying ebb and flow of unity and variety, not in the analytical sense meant by Hans Keller,[22] with its uncovering of latent
motivic connections between apparently diverse surface elements,
but aesthetically, as an overtly appreciable network of interrela-
tionships among themes flitting across the musical surface, and
functioning as a kind of 'narrative plot' to be read. Counter-
pointed against this narrative is another, cyclical one: the inner
movements represent a (temporary) departure from
monothematic unity, which returns, providing a sense of clo-

---

[21] For a detailed investigation, see Sutcliffe, *op. cit.*, pp. 87-8.
[22] For instance, 'The Chamber Music' in *The Mozart Companion* ed. H.C.
Robbins Landon and Donald Mitchell (London: Faber, 1956), pp. 90-137.

sure, in the finale.

As a final illustration, in which at least one aspect of the overarching balance of a four-movement quartet may be traced back to the consequences of Haydn's treatment of the opening theme, consider the G major quartet, op. 77 no. 1. The theme is a classic antecedent-consequent pair (I-V; V-I). As early as b. 4, Haydn fragments its dotted component as a 'space-filler', leading to the consequent portion. But at b. 14 ff. he manipulates it in a more potent fashion, assigning it to the cello (bb. 15 and 17) as an echo in a position widely separated from the rest of the ensemble at the bottom of the bass stave. This new spatial dimension cannot but provoke us to expect dialogue to feature prominently in the continuation, and from b. 27, the layout returns, inverted (the first violin now isolated in high register). This passage is a 'mirror' of b. 15 ff. and is, in effect, the 'second subject' in this monothematic sonata-form movement. Spatial separation of this dotted pattern, focusing respectively on 'low' and 'high' tessitura is an element of the exposition to which Haydn subsequently devotes considerable attention throughout the very long development (at bb. 87-100). However, it is absent from the recapitulation, which is substantially reconfigured, the section at bb. 14-45 of the exposition being omitted.

The absence of so prominent a textural feature may be felt as something of an imbalance in the structure of this movement. Read in terms of the entire quartet, however, it may be recognised instead as a withholding of resolution which it is the function of other movements to supply. As it happens, the antiphonal positioning of 'low' and 'high' tessitura, or else prominent registral separation, is remarkably prominent in the rest of the work, for instance:

Adagio, bb. 9-12; 16-20; 35-7; 44-6; 65-9

Minuet and Trio, bb. 8-11; 29-32; 43-53; 86-91; 96-102; 164-80

Finale, bb. 30-9; 60-2; 78-82; 86-9; 90-3; 108-17; 152-65; 232-49; 250-74

Such a reading would suggest that in op. 77 no. 1 Haydn achieves a synthesis of thematic design (principally its intervallic and rhythmic aspects), thematic manipulation, registral and textural contrast, and global structural fulfilment, the especially high incidence of quickfire antiphony in the finale serving simultaneously as culmination and resolution of implicit processes. The extent to which such a reading reflects authorial practice as embodied in a notated text, or whether it is simply an aspect of the work's meaning contributed by the reader (which, though imposed from without, may still be a valid stratum of its identity), it is the purpose of the remainder of this chapter to explore.

COUNTERPOINT AND INTERTEXTUALITY: FRAMEWORKS OF UNDERSTANDING

On one level, the fugal finales to op. 20 nos. 2, 5 and 6 may be appreciated in a purely structuralist fashion, that is, in terms of the supreme technical and compositional mastery that regulates their internal workings. On another level, one that extends beyond the individual movement (even beyond the individual work), these fugal finales inhabit a portion of the entirety of contrapuntal writing to be found amid Haydn's string quartets. Rigorous contrapuntal textures (and specifically imitative ones) are found both before and after the op. 20 fugues. Historically situated, the op. 20 fugal finales may be pictured either as an early culmination of Haydn's striving to achieve thorough-going integration of the ensemble, or else as a staging-post from which further developments were launched, independently of recourse to actual fugues, for instance, in op. 33, composed, according to the composer's own sales-pitch "in a new and special way". In terms of Haydn's application of imitative counterpoint within the string quartets, these three fugal finales gain meaning not solely in an internal, structuralist sense, but also in relation to other contrapuntal quartet movements which, considered collectively, amount to a 'theme' running through his output in this genre over a span of nearly half a century. The op. 20 fugues are pieces in a jigsaw whose 'picture' is fragmented across the whole of Haydn's quartets.

Correlatively, his subsequent incorporation of counterpoint within, for instance, sonata-form developments retains a 'trace' or 'echo' of the op. 20 fugues. Returning, for a moment, to a historical position of counterpoint within Haydn's quartets, each incursion of counterpoint beyond op. 20 is a reminder that the composer previously needed to resort to full-blown fugue in order to achieve genuine equality among the four instruments. It is also a declaration of his eventual attainment of a more sophisticated mode of utterance that achieves a dynamic accommodation of baroque and classical idioms.

The application of counterpoint in Haydn's quartet textures assumes a far broader range than strict fugue after op. 20. Only a couple of illustrations will be noted here. In the course of the first movement of op. 54 no. 2 in C, counterpoint forms part of a process of thematic evolution. Bars 3-4 present a semiquaver pattern which acquires an arpeggiaic suffix at bb. 15-17, a development chromatically adapted at bb. 43-4. Within the development section the last stage in this progression out of the original shape is adapted to a contrapuntal environment, serving as an invertible countersubject at bb. 100-19, including, at bb. 111-12, a stretto entry. A second species of contrapuntal theme-countertheme pairing is illustrated by the 'second subject' of the first movement of the F major quartet, op. 77 no. 2 (b. 37). Here the second violin quotes (in the dominant) the opening phrase of the movement (or, at least, its first six notes) as a countertheme to the first violin's chromatically ascending cantilena. In the following phrase (b. 46) this contrapuntal network appears in a higher octave register and with the parts inverted. From this point, the echos of the 'first subject' appear with greater frequency, entries being dovetailed throughout the texture, into which a reminiscence of the cello's pedal pattern from b. 9 is inserted for good measure, before the whole dissolves in cadential high jinks marking the end of the exposition.

Of course, the theme-countertheme pairing with which this section commences is commonly understood as exemplifying Haydn's famous tendency towards monothematicism. Historically construed, it might also be read as an illustration of the wonderful economy of means with which the ageing genius gives life and breath to a sonata form. If the monothematicism that we read into Haydn's text was indeed his intention here, then it was given voice by means of a particular application of a contrapuntal technique, one whose meaning (to us) derives not just from this particular location *in isolation*, but also from the frameworks of understanding offered by contrapuntal textures found scattered throughout Haydn's quartets, his other instrumental and vocal compositions (both sacred and secular), contemporary works by other composers, older works by baroque composers, and so on. That is to say, the 'meaning' of this particular contrapuntal passage in op. 77 no. 2 is *multiple*, and derives from a conflation of text and context; its meaning is not 'essential' (not wholly explicable within the narrow confines of the notated score), but 'intertextual'. Likewise, the meaning of Haydn's assumed monothematic strategy here is intertextual, not limited to the particular moment. Most immediately, its meaning draws upon its situation in a quartet paired with the G major quartet, op. 77 no. 1, whose first movement, as noted above, is also monothematic.[23] If Haydn had completed all six projected quartets of this commission for Prince Lobkowitz,[24] monothematicism might have been a recurrent (even consciously 'organising') feature, as it evidently was in the six quartets making up op. 50.[25] Indeed, the monothematicism of op. 77 (and more specifically, of the contrapuntally-organised 'second subject' of op. 77 no. 2) acquires some of its meaning intertextually by association with the practice of op. 50.

A HIGHER UNITY?

One frequently encounters the claim that Haydn's quartets (or, at least, his mature quartets) achieve a remarkable synthesis whereby all four movements blend together in complementary ways to form a single entity. This facet of Haydn's creative genius has been highlighted in relation to the op. 50 quartets by Dean Sutcliffe, for instance.[26] Planning of the external design of Haydn's quartets is evident from the first: his opp. 1 and 2 each present a five-movement pattern symmetrically arranged (fast-minuet-slow-minuet-fast). When he settled later upon a four-movement pattern in op. 9 (a pattern from which he was never again to deviate in his quartets), careful attention to the arrangement of the externals was once again a prime concern. The sequence in op. 9 always places the minuet second, evidently because the first movements are typically only *moderato*, and to place a slow movement immediately afterwards would have resulted in an aesthetically unsatisfactory postponement of quicker tempi. In later quartets, the position of the minuet varies, either

---

[23] In fact, both op. 77 quartets feature monothematic first movements and finales.
[24] The torso of op. 103 is also apparently to be considered a part of this commission.
[25] Sutcliffe, *op. cit.*, pp. 53-104 *passim*.
[26] Sutcliffe, *op. cit.* This attitude also informs Michael Spitzer's treatment of finales in the present volume, in which the function of closure is interpreted as something inevitably set in train by narratives embedded in previous movements.

preceding or following the slow movement, depending on the
particular circumstances, a decision always motivated by the desire for a harmonious balance of tempi, keys and character
throughout the four movements.[27]
    Turning to a consideration of the internal factors underpin-
ning that harmonious balance, it is apparent that the technical
means by which Haydn's inter-movement relations are felt to be
governed are of two main types: complementarity and parody.
Complementary relations attain a satisfying whole by supplying
some characteristic that an earlier movement had lacked (or, depending upon how much credibility one invests in such holistic
prophecy, had deliberately withheld). Parody operates by means
of a creative re-interpretation of a feature present in an earlier
movement. Both types will be examined here in the context of a
work considerably undervalued in the Haydn literature, the C
major quartet, op. 9 no. 1.
    Complementary relations might operate on both a 'local' and
a 'global' scale. The most obvious illustration of the former in
this quartet comes in the Minuet and Trio, which complement
each other in their major-minor modality, but also in terms of
content, for whereas the Minuet's opening phrase (eventually
re-interpreted as a cadence at the end) is subjected to a variety of
fragmented sequential treatments, the ensuing Trio holds
obstinately to a repetitive rhythm-pattern marking out an
unremitting metrical regularity, only dissolving (contrapuntally)
at the close. Recognition of an alternation of two distinctive
characters shapes our perception of this single movement, which
is to say that Haydn has calculated that the time-scale here is
compact enough for a listener to grasp the duality underlying
his local narrative. But to what extent does its efficacy reside in
the listener's perceptive faculties, rather than in the score itself?
To what extent can such connections support a broader span,
within a four-movement structure? Concrete answers are
certainly problematic, and perhaps impossible, but some
suggestions, invoking both 'complementarity' and 'parody'
categories, will be tentatively advanced here.

---

[27] Compare David Young's discussion (p. 58) of Haydn's ordering of movements
(Ed.).

Arguably, it is in the outer movements that complementary connections make an impression on the global design. Moving at the level of the beat and sub-beat rather than the bar, the first movement (*Moderato*) relies on a somewhat flat-footed application of imitative counterpoint for its integration of texture (at bb. 14-17, 20-2, 43-7, 56-9 and 62-4), an oddly incongruous incursion of uniform baroque pacing into an otherwise up-to-date display of *Empfindsamkeit*. By contrast, the textures in the finale are mobile, entirely in keeping with the dance-like vitality of its thematic content. The exposition of this sonata-form movement is especially varied in its textural profile, beginning as a first violin solo, to which the remaining instruments are conjoined at the end of the phrase, first in unison and octaves, then in cadential harmony. Subsequent textures include antecedent-consequent pairings of the first violin against the lower strings; then against just second violin and viola (giving temporary added prominence to the upper register); later on the first violin dives into the middle of the texture (b. 30, decorated from b. 38). Whereas the first movement still hovers between baroque and classical idioms, the finale makes the decisive forward leap of faith. Although its thematic content is distinctive enough, the confident succession of varied textures underpinning its progress plays at least as significant a role here as motivic design and development, offering an impressive culmination to the C major quartet.

In terms of its developmental process, the finale offers a parody of selected features of the first movement. Both movements are in sonata form and both development sections offer a segmented approach, latching onto two motives from their respective expositions, each one treated in turn (first movement, b. 30, b. 43; finale, b. 63, b. 85). Both, too, are reliant on sequential extension, the finale's development reversing the first movement's scheme: whereas the second segment of the first movement's development features sequence, in the finale, it is the first segment that is sequentially arranged. A further connection between these two passages is their manipulation of phrase-length. Bar 44 of the first movement sprouts a chromatic suffix that lengthens the original figure at bb. 14-15 by two beats. Conversely, the opening phrase of the finale, when announced at the start of its development section, is substantially contracted, being diverted chromatically after four bars into the sequentially based b. 63 ff.[28]

The rising chromatic suffix at b. 44 of the first movement raises the issue of thematic parody as an overarching device in Haydn's quartets. Its appearance here, exposed at the top of the texture, is certainly prominent. Might its origin be traced to the *falling* chromatic scale outlined by the first violin in bb. 30^4-33? Is chromaticism to be interpreted as a melodic gesture that re-curs as a 'fingerprint' across the surface of later movements of op. 9 no. 1, for example, in the minuet, bb. 13-14 (second vio-lin); in the *Adagio*, bb. 62-3; in the finale, at bb. 10-12 (first vio-lin), and many subsequent references to this figure? If so, what are the acceptable boundaries for recognising such a fingerprint? Could it extend, for instance, to b. 54 of the *Adagio* (an inverted adaptation); or to the main theme of the trio (a more remote relationship)? Or are such networks of correspondence actually the products of certain ways of thinking (or hearing), rather than inherent properties of the music? Indeed, are any of the factors underlying complementarity or parody 'essences', that is, signifying features of the music *itself*, in which a dimension of its coherence resides? Or are they phantoms, residing instead in analytical approaches designed to support an *a priori* assump-tion that Haydn's quartets are valorised (in part) insofar as they exhibit an overarching meta-narrative?

That such interconnections are to be taken for granted, in-deed, regarded as evidence of Haydn's developing genius, is a powerful *topos* in the Haydn literature. Thus Dean Sutcliffe:

> The individual work was now to be understood as a whole con-sisting of four parts rather than as a succession of musical 'num-bers', and this indeed represents the most profound change be-tween the early quartets and op. 9. The achievement of a higher unity, so that one multi-faceted idea seems to rule each work, is not just a matter of material connections between the movements but involves achieving characteristic sonorities and proportions that will only define the behaviour of one particular work.[29]

---

[28] The conceptual pairing of phrase extension/contraction might be felt to belong within the 'complementarity', rather than 'parody' category. Perhaps in a deep sense, both categories are founded upon the notion of re-interpretation, the former of character, the latter of process. More fundamentally, the categories themselves arguably reflect principles of cognition, rather than the recognition of essential musical attributes. On that measure, interpretation becomes something of a chi-mera as we chase our vanishing subjects, but we have to begin somewhere.

[29] Sutcliffe, *op. cit.*, p. 8.

Such a view invests heavily in the concept of a musical 'work' as something 'concrete', represented by a 'text', that has a particular identity capable of revelation by means of some or other analytical system (or performance). Or should that be a 'work-cum-text' that *needs to be given* a particular identity in order that it may conform to our inherited habits of mind whereby a 'great' work is one that 'achieves a higher unity'? Perhaps this powerful *topos* within Haydn studies is simply a particular application of an even more fundamental *topos* that 'greatness is unity'.

Historically contextualised, that *topos* feeds into another, yet more deeply situated, that of 'progress', typically expressed as a beginning-middle-end paradigm, according to which Haydn first composed quartets made up of 'a succession of musical numbers' so characteristic of the mid-eighteenth-century divertimento; next, he *achieved* 'a higher unity' (that is, such works represent an advance in sophistication over previous ones); finally, his later quartets (such as op. 50, which are the main subject of Sutcliffe's investigation) are characterised by the most profound and subtle interconnections between the four movements, elements that "define the behaviour of [the] particular work".

In the E flat quartet, op. 64 no. 6, for example, these 'defining elements' may be said to include the incorporation of remote tonalities as poles of extreme emotional contrast. In the first movement, the development modulates widely, reaching G flat at b. 84 (a so-called 'false reprise'); this tonal flux is parallelled in the central passage of the *Andante*, ranging through B flat minor, D flat, A flat minor and E flat minor. More important, perhaps, as a controlling element in this quartet is the cross-referencing of contrapuntal textures. The first-movement development is almost entirely regulated by either stretto imitations or else by antiphonal textures involving theme-countertheme pairings. Each of the subsequent movements likewise features counterpoint strongly: the outer sections of the *Andante*; the trio, in which something of the stretto and antiphonal textures of the first movement are recaptured; and the second episode in the finale, bb. 91-140. The relationship between the contrapuntal sections of the outer movements is arguably very strong, since in each case the principal thematic material is shown in a new light. Possibly, there is a 'metrical' cross-relation, too. Both the first movement and the finale conclude with a progressively accelerated cadential figure sounded by the first violin at the top of the texture above chordal punctuation from the rest of the ensemble (first movement, bb. 140-4; finale, bb. 178-92).

How applicable such interconnections truly are in Haydn's quartets must remain an open question in the absence of specific positive documentary evidence, for example, in Haydn's correspondence (to the effect that he intended such cross-referencing), or else in his autographs (such as revisions introducing an obvious link to another movement where none previously existed). Certainly, some of the alleged thematic resemblances through which separate movements of Haydn's quartets are supposed to be brought into synthesis appear to have little more than wishful thinking to recommend them. Only relatively rarely, as in the case of bb. 49-56 and 178-85 in the finale of op. 50 no. 6, is the resemblance to a previous movement obvious (in this case the opening of the quartet's first movement evoked by correlation of instrument, register, note-values, interval-shape, and even precise pitch).

Returning to instances of parody in op. 9 no. 1, arguably a more convincing level of reinterpretation than the purely thematic is to be found within the finale, namely the application of variation, not as a genre, but as a technique imported into, in this case, a sonata form. There are both 'local' and 'structural' variants on show here. An obvious example of the former is the immediate decoration of the first violin pattern of bb. 30-3 in semiquavers at bb. 38-41. A memorable illustration of the latter is the manner in which Haydn recasts the transition (bb. 18-30) towards the finale's close. Instead of simply repeating the falling suspension-chain of bb. 24-7, he reconfigures it so that the falling steps are transferred from second to first violin and incorporated within an extension of the prevailing rhythm pattern (bb. 122-5). Thereafter, the original roles of first and second violins are exchanged in bb. 130-42. Perhaps the most telling variant is a textural one. The moment of recapitulation is brought unforgettably into focus by being sounded by the full ensemble (intervallically adapted), in contrast to the unsupported entry of the first violin at b. 1 and b. 57. Such reinterpretations, or parodies, of earlier passages play a crucial role in the dynamic unfolding of this brilliant finale.

Reading this finale as an exhibition of variation practices does not, of course, afford an escape from the *impasse* between authorial intentionality *versus* interpretation. Like all of the other approaches touched on earlier in this chapter, its authority resides both in Haydn's intentions as embodied in his scores and in inherited traditions of intellectual enquiry. Neither side can lay claim to full, exclusive 'presence'; instead, each depends on the other for a part of its truth. Those singular expressive entities that we recognise as Haydn string quartets occupy a space midway between the composer's conscious technical processes and the historical procession of responses (including our own).[30] While the composer can control the former, he cannot legislate for the latter agencies through which his quartets continue, and will continue, to speak.

[30] And even to configure it thus is to admit a degree of historical contingency, alluded to in Dahlhaus's discussion mentioned in note 7 above.

II

The First Movements

Denis McCaldin

INTRODUCTION

No composer of the eighteenth century drew more from his exploitation of the sonata principle that Joseph Haydn. The range and ingenuity of his response to its elegant single underlying idea is remarkable. To find a similar level of prolific inventiveness, it is necessary to go back to J. S. Bach's achievement in respect of his church cantatas. In those works, the baroque master adapted and expanded a variety of different procedures within a single compositional formula for his weekly contribution to the Lutheran rite. And although part of Bach's creative response certainly arose from his own ingenuity, part must also have been informed by his deep knowledge of the liturgy and the text appropriate to the annual church calendar.

By comparison, Haydn created a similarly large body of work but his achievement is all the more striking because so much of his music is without voices. Formally, his instrumental music – the symphonies, keyboard sonatas, trios and string quartets – cannot rely on structures dictated by a text, and so has to stand on its own. Consequently, the composer's dependence on formal procedures, and particularly on the sonata principle, became central. Nowhere is this more apparent than in the string quartets.

The focus of this chapter is on the first movements, where Haydn's inventive use of the sonata principle is at its most varied. Particular attention is given here to op. 1 no. 1, op. 17 no. 4, op. 33 no. 2, op. 64 no. 5 and op. 76 no. 4. The aim is to study the progress of Haydn's quartet style in a medium to which he seems to have been attracted in part because of its potential for abstract musical thought. Furthermore, it is particularly in the first movements that he seems to have relished the prospect of redefining and exploring the formal idea of the sonata principle.

DEFINITIONS OF THE SONATA PRINCIPLE

Among many definitions of the so-called first-movement sonata principle, two of the most useful are those of Charles Rosen and James Webster. In *The Classical Style*, Rosen states:

> Since Czerny, the sonata has been most often defined as a melodic structure. ...the exposition starts with a theme or group of themes in the tonic followed by a modulation to the dominant and a second group of themes; after a repetition of the exposition comes the development, in which the themes are fragmented and combined in various keys ending with a return to the tonic and a recapitulation of the exposition, this time with the second group of themes in the tonic, and an optional coda.[1]

James Webster offers a somewhat more technical perspective of sonata form in *The New Grove Dictionary of Music and Musicians*. He begins:

> A typical sonata-form movement consists of a two-part tonal structure, articulated in three main sections. The first part of the structure coincides with the first section and is called the 'exposition'. The second part of the structure comprises the remaining two sections, the 'development' and the 'recapitulation'.

He further states:

> Sonata form is a synthesis of binary and ternary principles: it integrates three sections in a two-part structure. Sonata form is bipartite, in that the exposition has the same tonal structure as a half-cadence or the first half of a binary form: it is open, poised on the dominant, tonally incomplete .[2] [Ex. 1]

Ex.1 (from *The New Grove*, p. 497)

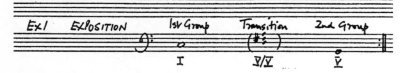

Hence it requires resolution by a balancing second part (the development and recapitulation) which closes in the tonic. The central aesthetic event of the entire movement is a return to the main theme within the second part, timed to arrive simultaneously with the return to the tonic. Neither a simple restatement of the main theme or a simple return to the tonic has the intense

---

[1] Charles Rosen and James Webster, *The Classical Style* (London: Faber & Faber, 1971), p. 30.
[2] James Webster in *The New Grove Dictionary of Music and Musicians* (London: Macmillan, 1980), p. 497.

impact of this 'double return'. [Ex. 2]

Ex. 2 (from *The New Grove*, p. 498 – diagram modified)

With these definitions in mind, let us consider one of Haydn's earliest quartets.

OP. 1 NO. 1 IN B FLAT ('LA CHASSE')

This work is one of a group of some ten quartets, most probably written between 1757 and 1762, which Haydn described as 'divertimenti'. The fact that this example is the first of the opus 1 grouping is perhaps less important than that it shows the starting point for the composer's development of the genre during the remainder of his working life.

Modern research continues to throw fresh light on Haydn's early years and the compositions dating from them. One particular influence at this time, when the composer was in his late teens and early twenties, arose through domestic music making. According to Griesinger[3], Haydn was asked by one of his early patrons Baron Fürnberg, who owned an estate at Weinzierl outside Vienna, to write something for four stringed instruments that he and another musician Albrechtsberger could play with the Baron's estates' manager and his local priest to entertain the household. Haydn's acceptance led to the composition of op. 1 no. 1 and its companion pieces.

Scholars have naturally sought to find other precursors for Haydn's 'first string quartets'. One in particular is the string trio (for two violins and bass), of which the composer wrote at least thirty-four in these same early years. But their diversity of

---

[3] Quoted in H.C. Robbins Landon, *Haydn Chronicle and Works: The Early Years* (London: Thames and Hudson, 1980), p. 228.

style is in strong contrast to the consistent language of the early quartets. A more fruitful line of descent is from the Viennese open-air serenades and cassations, many of which Haydn performed as a freelance player in the years following his expulsion from the choir at St. Stephen's cathedral. As street music, these divertimenti had to be attractive, with lively rhythms, catchy melodies and simple forms. Above all, they had to be sturdily portable, using textures that would sound well outdoors, without either *basso continuo* support or full instrumentation.

One of the defining features of Haydn's ten early quartets which links them to this model is the consolidation of a pattern of movements typical of the divertimento. Eight of these quartets have a symmetrical cluster of five movements around a central lyrical *Adagio* which is flanked on either side by a minuet and an *Allegro* or *Presto* at the beginning and the end. This is the pattern in op. 1 no. 1, whose opening movement is now examined in more detail.

Although it is tempting to see too much of a composer's mature language in his earliest pieces, some aspects of a personal voice are always present and Haydn is no exception. In the first movement of the op. 1 no. 1 quartet, there are features of the form, melody, harmony, rhythm and texture that prefigure much that is to come.

Exposition

Even in such a short movement of some sixty-two bars, Haydn's formal control contributes substantially to the listener's pleasure, along with the sturdy 6/8 'hunting' rhythm and the uncluttered melodic shapes. The twenty-four-bar exposition shows three clear sections, each, incidentally, with its own rhythmic character. It begins with opening octave-based phrases (Theme 1, bb. 1-8, B flat major), followed by a transition section in quavers (Transition, bb. 9-16, F major) and a concluding semiquaver-dominated passage (Cadential Theme 2, bb. 17-24, F major).

Development and Recapitulation

For the development section (sixteen bars), Haydn continues with the Cadential Theme 2 and arrives at the recapitulation via *fortissimo* octaves in the tonic minor (bb. 37-8). This double return (b. 41) uses shortened versions of both Theme 1 and the Transition in the tonic and is followed by a complete restatement of the Cadential Theme in the home key of B flat major. [Ex. 3]

Ex. 3 Diagram of op. 1, no. 1, I

The underlying structural principles that are subsequently to show a fascinating diversity in Haydn's later quartets can be seen here with helpful simplicity. [Ex. 4] Other features of the composer's embryonic quartet style already evident in this work are the strong rhythmic drive and variety of instrumental textures, along with the use of

i) octave passages – especially in the context of 'question and answer' where the reply is harmonised in several parts (bb. 1-4);
ii) dynamic contrast – as in the *forte/piano* exchanges of the opening bars;
iii) silences – especially here at the recapitulation (b. 40).

Ex. 4 op. 1 no. 1, I, bb. 1-24 (Exposition) [CD 1]

Haydn initially joined Prince Nikolaus Esterházy's staff in 1761 and was made full Kapellmeister five years later. Although the Prince required a steady flow of works of all kinds, his interest in instrumental music was centred mainly on baryton trios and symphonies composed specifically for the Esterházy court and which remained the Prince's property. Haydn was always anxious to secure a wider audience, and may well have believed that because string quartets were not required for official court music-making, works written in that genre offered an opportunity to reach a new and wider public. This is one possible explanation for the composition of his op. 9 quartets which he entered in his catalogue around 1770. By this time, his instrumental style was becoming more technically integrated. He himself observed that these were his first real string quartets. What Haydn began to discover in these works seems to have been important because within the next two years he went on to compose two more sets: opp. 17 and 20.

The op. 9 group dates from the beginning of this fruitful period. The number of movements is now reduced to four by omitting the second minuet of the old divertimento model. The first movement is generally the most expansive and experimental, offering more equal interest to all four players both in terms of thematic treatment and more elaborate part-writing (as in op. 9 no. 1).

OP. 17 NO. 4 IN C MINOR

The progression towards a quartet style involving all four players is further explored in the op. 17 quartets of 1771. Rosemary Hughes credits Friedrich Blume with the idea that in these works

> ... the unity of all four movements, thematic and spiritual, is far closer than in op. 9, and in the first movements, the process of developing the principal themes is not confined to the middle section, traditionally called the development, but begins to develop *from the moment of their inception* [this author's italics].[4]

This ability to realise so many implications from the smallest and simplest of ideas, and to weave them into expressive and satisfying structures lies at the heart of Haydn's greatness as a composer of string quartets. Increasingly, whole movements stem from a single motive, and this interest in monothematicism, which remained a feature of his maturing style, is particularly well defined in the first movement of op. 17 no. 4. [CD 2]

Exposition

The crucial thematic idea in this movement consists of three minims and is announced by the first violin alone (b. 1). There is a playful ambiguity of expectation in that only when the cello enters in the second bar do we realise the home tonality is C minor and not E flat major. [Ex. 5]

Ex. 5
op. 17 no. 4, I, bb. 1-2

---

[4] *Haydn String Quartets* (London: BBC, 1966), p. 22.

Rather than delay discussion of this three-note motive until the development, Haydn immediately begins to explore its implications within the exposition. The most important of these are given below: [Ex. 6]

Ex. 6 op. 17 no. 4, I, bb. 9-10 and 20-1

b. 1	Theme	C minor
b. 9	Theme reharmonised	E flat major
b. 20	Transition (theme in cello) viola has diminution (bb. 27-30)	E flat major
b. 41	Cadential material (theme in diminution at b. 45)	E flat major

Development

Within this portion of the movement, the theme is now used as a kind of pivot with which the music is drawn through a range of tonalities.

b. 53	Theme with cello restatement (b. 60)	A flat major
b. 62	Theme	B flat minor
b. 76	Cadential material	C minor

At b. 78, the music is extended by three wonderfully effective dramatic devices which delay the recapitulation and so create extra tension. The first is a brief questioning silence, followed by a remarkable canonic section that looks almost like an extract from a seventeenth-century motet (b. 79) which then leads via a 'false' statement in E flat (b. 86) to the recapitulation itself (b. 92). [Ex. 7]

Ex. 7 op. 17 no. 4, I, bb. 53-54, 62-3 and 76-86
(facing)

bb. 53-54

bb. 62-63

bb. 76-86

Recapitulation

After such intense thematic manipulation, the recapitulation proceeds more conventionally. The main idea and its transition occupy less than half the number of bars in the exposition while the cadential section (b. 108) is transposed unchanged except in tonality. The brief coda (bb. 120-130) is one more feature of the sonata principle which Haydn began to explore about this time. It starts boldly, with a rhetorical version of the theme in octaves [Ex. 8] before the music subsides *mancando* to *pianissimo*, with

semiquavers in the inner voices counterpointing gently with the
motivically-derived minims of the first violin.

b. 92	Theme	C minor
b. 108	Cadential material	C minor
b. 120	Coda (theme)	C minor

Ex. 8 op. 17 no. 4, I, bb. 120-3

In conclusion, it is clear that in both his op. 9 and op. 17,
Haydn was already fascinated with the flexibility of the sonata
principle and its possibilities. The deepening of his musical style
is apparent throughout these twelve quartets. In this first movement of op. 17 no. 4, we can also appreciate the dramatic use of
silence (bb. 9, 42, 78) and of a wider dynamic range, as in the
coda. Some problems of rhythm and texture remain; the chug-
ging cello line and dominant first violin part (notably in the
development section) are features of an earlier style which tend
to hamper the flow of the musical conversation. As Charles Rosen
suggests:

> Haydn's style of 1770, while it had taken account of the develop-
> ment, was not yet able to embrace its full implications. The higher
> degree of articulation of phrase and polarity of harmony raised
> problems of continuity that were difficult to solve: the shapes
> and rhythms move without transition from the squarely regular
> to the unsystematic, relying in the latter case almost entirely on
> repetition or upon Baroque sequences to justify the sense of mo-
> tion.[5]

Nevertheless, Haydn's achievement in devising a genuine string-
quartet style is clearly evident in the op. 17 quartets and is con-
solidated in those of op. 20 composed a year later.

---

[5] Rosen & Webster, *op. cit.*, p. 146.

Op. 33 No. 2 in E flat ('The Joke')

It seems likely that Haydn's intense period of quartet composition in the early 1770s may be linked in some way with the changes that were taking place in his personal life around this time. Although the next few years were more fallow, by 1781, the composer seems to have recovered his enthusiasm for quartet writing with the announcement of a set of six known as op. 33. These were published by Artaria in Vienna in April 1782, and Haydn's letter offering pre-publication manuscript copies by subscription demonstrates both his belief in their quality and his commercial acumen. The one written to the Swiss writer, J. C. Lataver, begins:

> I love and happily read your works. As one reads, hears and relates, I am not without adroitness myself, since my name (as it were) is known and highly appreciated in every country. I am issuing, by subscription, for the price of 6 ducats, a work, consisting of 6 Quartets for 2 violins, viola and violoncello *concertante* correctly copied, and WRITTEN IN A NEW AND SPECIAL WAY (FOR I HAVE NOT COMPOSED ANY FOR 10 YEARS).[6]

The precise meaning of the last sentence in this letter has given rise to much speculation. One thing that is clearly discernible in op. 33 is a broadening of the scope of each individual movement. The minuets are now entitled *scherzo* or *scherzando*, the slow movements have a meditative spaciousness, while the finales show some further exploration following the fugal experiments of the op. 20 scores.

But in terms of a new quartet style it is the element of equality between the four instrumentalists that has now become central to the musical syntax. The first part of Haydn's message to his would-be subscribers, where he describes the four parts as *concertante*, suggests that he believed he was still developing his interest in contrapuntal textures, following his experiments in the op. 20 quartets. As David Schroeder says:

> The primary appeal of the quartet was to the players, and this had a strong bearing on the musical procedures used, such as the nature of the counterpoint... The contrapuntal process of the quartets tends to be one of expanding a single motive, reflecting the potential equality of the parts (or performers)... Motivic expansion is taken further in quartets [than symphonies], and one

[6] Quoted in W. Dean Sutcliffe, *Haydn String Quartets, op. 50* (Cambridge: Cambridge University Press, 1992), p. 18.

could argue, constitutes their essence.[7]

This concentration on musical conversation between equals is clearly evident in the first movement of op. 33 no. 2. [CD 3]

Exposition

As in op. 17 no. 4 above, Haydn's interest in monothematicism remains important and, in the first movement of this quartet, the main musical material is derived from the opening two bars (see Ex. 9 below). The principal idea is again a three-note motive, heard initially in the first violin. However, the mode of treatment is more complex. Melodically it is even simpler and consists simply of a rising fourth. But the strong rhythmic character of its two upbeat semiquavers turns out to be the driving force for much that follows. Whereas in op. 17 no. 4, the motive was most often used linearly, as a kind of pivot to send the musical argument in fresh directions, here Haydn explores his material using the four instruments architecturally from the beginning. In the first eight bars alone, the textural changes in the answering phrase (bb. 5-8) already point to "the new and special way". [Ex. 9]

Ex. 9 op. 33 no. 2, I, bb. 1-8

---

[7] David Schroeder, *Haydn and the Enlightenment: the Late Symphonies and their Audience* (Oxford: Clarendon Press, 1990), p. 62.

Similarly, the equivalent part of the next eight-bar phrase draws all four players into the discussion, beginning with the cellist (b. 12). The tonality moves to the dominant at b. 21 (transition) and for eight bars, the music is more harmonically conceived, using a melodic ornament and semiquaver septuplets. After such detailed working out within the exposition, and in view of what he wished to explore in the development, Haydn may have sensed the need to break away from too much dependence on his theme by introducing this more relaxed episode. The cadential material then returns to the main theme (b. 29).

b. 1	Theme	E flat
b. 21	Transition	B flat
b. 29	Cadential (based on Theme)	B flat

Development

Contrapuntal dialogue features strongly here, beginning with brief exchanges between cello and first violin and proceeding canonically with the viola (b. 35) and later the cello (b. 39). Further motivic working out via the remote tonality of D flat leads to a cadential flourish and silence (b. 58). A 'false' recapitulation in C minor (as in op. 17 no. 4, b. 86) again delays the return to the home key and a second silence (b. 62) further heightens expectation.

Recapitulation

Following such detailed exploration in the two earlier sections of this monothematic movement, Haydn opts for a relaxed recapitulation, excising eight bars (bb. 9-16) from the exposition, and transposing the transition and cadential material into E flat. The temptation to continue the discussion with a coda is resisted.

Even a brief glance at this score reveals that as well as strength-

ening the coherence of the motivic argument in this movement,
Haydn shows a growing interest in introducing more rhythmic
variety as well. This is particularly true of the Transition material where syncopations, ornamental turns and triplet/sextuplet
figuration offer the listener some relaxation. In broader, more
philosophical terms, David Schroeder describes another dimension that Haydn was beginning to explore:

> In the string quartets, and in a heightened way with op. 33, the
> music places four intelligent people in a 'harmonious' setting,
> sharing both intellectual and heartfelt experience... In a very real
> way, then, the quartet became a realisation of one of the highest
> goals of the Enlightenment. With accompaniments that can be
> transformed into melodies and *vice versa*, there is an apparent
> recognition of a higher social truth which is that differences do
> not preclude equality.[8]

OP. 64 NO. 5 IN D ('THE LARK')

When the op. 64 quartets appeared in 1791, Haydn was fifty-
eight. The years immediately following the publication of op.
33 had been much concerned with domestic opera production
for the Esterházys and this affected the composer's work in other
genres. Of the quartets written during the following decade,
Hans Keller notes the high quality of the neglected op. 42, whose
first movement again explores elements of monothematicism.
Similarly, the external commission from Cadiz for *The Seven
Last Words* (1787) provided a compositional challenge which
Haydn met with characteristic inventiveness. The rich variety
of the op. 50 quartets from the same year is discussed in fascinating detail in the recent monograph by Dean Sutcliffe.[9]

Two further sets of six quartets op. 54-5 and op. 64, generally
known as the 'Tost' quartets, followed in the years 1788-90. By
this time, Haydn was probably the most celebrated composer in
Europe, and while for most of his working life he had been
obliged to compose to order, he was now free to choose from
the many offers of patronage outside the Esterházy court. The
commission from Johann Tost would have been particularly ap-
pealing. Tost had been a violinist in Haydn's orchestra before

[8] *ibid.*, p. 62.
[9] Sutcliffe, *op. cit.*

marrying into money and becoming a travelling Viennese busi-
nessman. He was undoubtedly a talented player – to judge from
the *moto perpetuo* finale of this fifth quartet of the op. 64 set –
and Haydn would have been keen to provide his former colleague with appropriate technical challenges. But rather than
simply produce a series of *quattuor brilliants*, with the three lower
instruments simply supporting a virtuosic first violin part, Haydn
chose to integrate this new element into his existing quartet style.
Mention has been made already of the finale of this quartet,
where, as Hans Keller says "...the leader's [joy] springs from
him having it both ways – virtuosically and easily".[10] In the first
movement, too, Haydn appears to take particular delight in the
freedom offered by Tost's abilities to extend and exploit the range
of the first violin part.

Exposition [CD 4]

One of the most characteristic features of the opening movement of this 'Lark' quartet, so-called because of the high tessitura
and birdsong-like ornamentation of its opening theme, is its spaciousness. Such is Haydn's control over his musical material that
whereas in op. 33 no. 2 the opening *Allegro moderato* has ninety
bars, here the same tempo indication is used for a movement of
some 179 measures.

In structural terms, the movement is not monothematic. Instead, Haydn makes a virtue out of contrast in the exposition by
polarising the D major serenity of the first group's accompaniment (b. 1) and high violin melody (b. 9) [Ex. 10] with some
chromatically rich syncopation in the second (transition) group
(b. 35). [Ex. 11] The tension which this causes so early on in the
movement cleverly establishes an element of conflict which is
only partially resolved later in the cadential passage (bb. 50-9),
[Ex. 12] where the rhythm becomes more stable, the chromaticism less disruptive and the musical discussion arrives firmly at
the double bar in the dominant tonality of A major.

[10] *ibid.*, p. 164.

Ex. 10 op. 64 no. 5, I, bb. 1-12 (Theme)

Ex. 11 op. 64 no. 5, I, bb. 35-42 (Transition)

Ex. 12 op. 64 no. 5, I, bb. 50-9 (Cadential)

Development

The wealth of contrasting material within the exposition is considered in the development section with apparently natural

assurance. It begins with a Haydnesque ambiguity. For a moment (b. 60), the listener is uncertain whether the music will
move onto the subdominant. That it does, and with such ease, is
mainly achieved by the simple device of converting the former
quavers of the opening (see Ex. 10), into *legato* crotchets. [Ex. 13,
b. 62 *et seq.*] Thereafter, the development is expansive rather
than turbulent, moving through some eighty bars of varied textures which show many of the characteristics of Haydn's mature
style – contrasting *piano/forte* dynamics, silences, and a *fortissimo* unison passage leading to an extended 'false reprise' of the
movement's opening idea (b. 106).

Ex. 13 op. 64 no. 5, I, bb. 60-4

Recapitulation

After the spaciousness of the development, the recapitulation
is highly compact. Characteristically, Haydn includes some re-
working of the fifty-nine bar exposition which is now reduced
to thirty-seven. Notable are the second violin's continuous quavers under the so-called 'lark' theme (b. 142) which relate back,
almost like punctuation marks, to the beginning of both previous sections (b. 1, b. 60) of this exceptionally lucid sonata-form
movement.

This work by Haydn, one of the most famous in the quartet
literature, is admired by both listeners and performers, and it is
easy to be deceived by the subtle simplicity of this first movement. By the time it was written, Haydn seems to have forged a
quartet style that could illuminate even the most intractable of
ideas. As this quartet shows, his melodies have now become sup-
ple, polyrhythmic and idiomatic. Perhaps in response to Mozart,
the harmony too is now more strongly tinged with chromaticism than before, and the rhythms more varied. Most successful

of all is the discovery of a wider range of textures involving all four players in music that has both clarity and spaciousness.

OP. 76 NO. 4 IN B FLAT ('THE SUNRISE')

During the last decade of the eighteenth century, Haydn's standing changes from his relatively obscure position at the Esterházy court to that of a composer of international stature. Moreover, by the time the Tost quartets were completed in 1790, the composer's circumstances were about to be transformed by the death of his patron Prince Nikolaus and an invitation from Salomon to visit London.

The next two sets of quartets, opp. 71 and 74 (six in all) were dedicated to Count Apponyi and were written during Haydn's time back in Vienna between his two English visits of 1791 and 1795. They are works of rich diversity and show the influence of the composer's new celebrity and his bond with his British audience. However, this study concludes with a consideration of the fourth of the op. 76 set [CD 5] which, together with the two examples which constitute op. 77, make up the composer's final contributions to a genre central to his place in musical history.

It was probably in 1796, shortly after Haydn had returned to Vienna for the last time, that Count Erdödy commissioned the six op. 76 quartets. In spite of advancing age, the next few years continued to be productive. As well as completing the two oratorios and the six great masses, Haydn's publishers were constantly pressing him for new works or revised versions of earlier ones. What energy that remained for instrumental composition was focused on the quartets rather than the symphonies and piano sonatas that London had inspired.

Exposition

The extra dimension that can be detected in these last chamber works of Haydn's maturity arises in part from their performance at public concerts. For the marathon events of the 1790s in the Hanover Square Rooms and elsewhere, concert programmes were extremely varied, with orchestral items juxtaposed between solo and chamber music of many different kinds. The challenge for Haydn in his op. 71 and the quartets that followed was to redefine his musical language to suit such performing spaces. Part of this new vocabulary was the use of strong rhetorical gestures and richer sonorities. A fine example can be seen

at the end of the exposition and recapitulation of this quartet
where Haydn uses 'quasi-orchestral' writing to maximise the volume of sound. [Ex. 14]

Ex. 14 op. 76 no. 4, I, bb. 66-7

In this work, nicknamed 'The Sunrise' after the ascending
shape of the opening violin theme, Haydn appears to retain his
interest in monothematicism but at a different level. Taking the
quartet as a whole, the motive of a semitone plus a third unifies
all four movements. [Ex. 15] What is striking in these late quartets is the variety of formal treatment of the first movements.

Ex. 15 op. 76 no. 4 bb. 1-2 (first violin) of each movement

Only a master would be able to build a wholly convincing monothematic structure from the two falling intervals of 'The Fifths'
quartet op. 76 no. 2. In 'The Sunrise', it is the first violin's extraordinary long-limbed rising melody that Haydn uses as the
principal subject for a different kind of monothematicism. En-
compassing the interval of a twelfth, and concluding at the end
of six bars with three points of silence, the stillness of the lower
instruments' sustained chord beneath allows the listener to concentrate on the character of the theme both in this statement and

its immediate answer. Thereafter, this characterful theme appears in different forms at strategic points throughout the movement.

The same expansiveness that was noted in respect of the exposition of 'The Lark' quartet op. 64 no. 5 is taken further here. In each of the first two phrases, the harmonic rhythm remains static for four complete bars before moving to the cadence, producing a tranquil opening paragraph of reflective calm. This contrasts well with the vigorous passagework of the transition which follows (b. 22). Although there is much activity, the harmony continues to move at a leisurely pace, ensuring that the relaxed mood of the opening is not disturbed. Hans Keller rightly drew attention to this almost pastoral serenity in relation to a later work by Haydn's most illustrious pupil, noting that "with its gradual evolution, the structure foreshadows the first movement of Beethoven's first 'Rasumovsky' Quartet op. 59 no. 1."[11]

Equality of treatment for all four instruments is again apparent in the theme's third statement (b. 12) where motivic material that might previously have been assigned exclusively to the first violin is shared with the viola. Such detail goes beyond the purely democratic textures of earlier works to embrace a heightened concern for instrumental colour. [Ex. 16]

Ex. 16 op. 76 no. 4, I, bb. 1-15

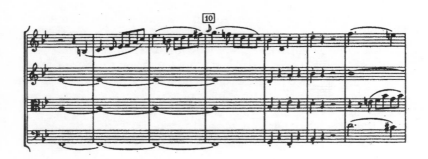

As well as the familiar tonal contrast between tonic and dominant in Haydn's mature sonata form movements, the tonal shift is often enhanced by introducing the dominant with powerfully contrasting material. So it is here, where loud 'busywork' for the whole ensemble creates a dramatic diversion (b. 22) before the expected restatement of the 'Sunrise' theme in the dominant F major. At this point, Haydn produces the first of several ingenious touches. Instead of simply restating the main theme in the new tonality, it now appears on the cello *in inversion* and in a more condensed form. So the motive that began the movement as a six-bar theme is here presented upside down in three. [Ex. 17]

As Rosemary Hughes explains, "the whole paragraph grows outwards from the rhythm and melodic line of the melody with wonderful flexibility and continuity of phrase-structure and translucency of scoring".[12] A codetta (b. 50 ff.), based on contrasts of texture and dynamic, and balancing the earlier passagework

---

[12] *ibid.*, p. 50.

Ex. 17 op. 76 no. 4, I, bb. 37-40

(b. 22), concludes this elaborate exposition which is nevertheless cogently based on its opening melody and the two significant intervals (semitone and third) within it.

b. 1	Theme	B flat major
b. 22	Transition	B flat major
b. 37	Theme (inverted)	F major
b. 50	Cadential (codetta)	F major

Development

Perhaps to counterbalance the expansive character of the exposition which now characteristically already 'develops' the main material – see, for example, the *fz/p* section bb. 44-8 – the development section is short and based on a tripartite tonal scheme. Each of the differently textured elements of the exposition is discussed in a new key area. At the double bar, the tonality quits the dominant via a restatement of the 'Sunrise' theme, but with the harmony intensified through D minor and a diminished seventh on F sharp towards the submediant. The second section (b. 80 etc.), based on the Transition material, extends and consolidates this G minor tonality. The third Cadential paragraph (b. 96 etc.) is used to modulate to the dominant.

Recapitulation

As was later to be the case with Beethoven, Haydn continues to develop his ideas up to the end of the movement. The recapitulation opens with the 'Sunrise' theme in the tonic, but now accompanied by a *crescendo* and *forte* (not *piano*) cadential chords. At the expected reprise of the inverted version of the theme (b. 142) comes another ingenious twist. The cello phrase now rises, and then falls in even pairs of quavers, creating still more appoggiatura-derived dissonances than before. The 'orchestral' *fortissimo* that concluded the exposition is here interrupted by a held chord which then neatly dissolves into a short coda (b. 175), where the viola and second violin offer a brief afterthought before the final cadence.

CONCLUSION

Haydn's progress from his early quartets to the mature works of his later years shows him to have been a consummate musician. In the composition of the first movements, as elsewhere, it is fascinating to observe the range of his invention. His exploration of the sonata principle, and with it, his predilection for monothematic procedures, show the fertility of his remarkable mind. The few examples discussed here make up only a small part of the complete picture, but hopefully they are sufficient to indicate the nature of Haydn's contribution to the music of his time and in particular to the evolution of the string quartet.

III

The Slow Movements

David Young

Introduction

The present chapter considers the slow movements of Haydn's string quartets from the point of view of their *varied, experimental*, and *innovatory* nature. Less emphasis than usual in writings of this type is placed on chronological development, since the present writer does not find a steady growth from promising beginnings to ultimate perfection; rather he finds strokes of genius liberally distributed throughout Haydn's *oeuvre*. In short, the material in this chapter is organized as follows:

Number and order of slow movements;
Key and tonality;
Topics and expression;
Form.

'Slow movement' is, of course, a relative term, for, whereas the vast majority of movements under discussion have tempo marks which are recognisably 'slow' – that is, *Andante, Adagio*, or *Largo* or their derivatives – two are marked *Allegretto* (as in Beethoven's Eighth Symphony) or even *Allegretto scherzando* (op. 54 no. 1 and op. 64 no. 1).[1]

Number and Order

All sixty-eight string quartets under consideration have at least one slow movement. (Haydn's *Seven Last Words*, which consists of eight slow movements and a *Presto* finale, does not figure in this discussion since, as we know, this work was not originally conceived as a string quartet and the present concern is to relate the slow movements to the cycles as a whole.) Three quartets (op. 9 no. 5, op. 42, and op. 54 no. 2) have two slow movements each (see below, Table 1).

---

[1] The only 'slow' movement without a tempo mark is the third movement of op. 20 no. 1 (*Affetuoso e sostenuto*).

TABLE 1
String quartets with two slow movements

Op. 9 No. 5
Poco Adagio (theme and variations); Minuet and Trio; *Largo cantabile; Presto*

Op. 42
Andante, ed Innocentemente; Minuet and Trio; *Adagio, e Cantabile; Presto*

Op. 54 No. 2
Vivace; Adagio; Minuet and Trio; *Adagio-Presto-Adagio*

The first two examples in Table 1 follow a similar movement order to the old *sonata da chiesa*; however, the third example contains a highly innovative finale which is basically a slow movement with a central *Presto* section. (This mixing of slow and fast tempi in a finale anticipates Beethoven's op. 18 no. 6, although Beethoven's movement is rather different in that it ends quickly.)

The positioning of the slow movements (as analysed in Table 2 below) is by no means arbitrary. In eight out of ten of the five-movement cycles which make up opp. 1 and 2, the slow movement is placed third, making it, in terms of length, intensity of expression, as well as position, the centre of gravity. (In the remaining two cases, op. 1 no. 3 and op. 2 no. 6, the slow movement is placed first whilst the internal *da capo* fast movement is placed third – that is, Slow-Minuet and Trio-Fast-Minuet and Trio-Fast.) In opp. 9 and 17, because the first movements tend to be marked *Allegro Moderato* or *Moderato* (with exceptions – Haydn is not entirely uniform here), the slow movement (or, in the case of op. 9 no. 5, the second slow movement) is placed third, probably in order to ensure that strongly contrasted pairings pertain, in these cases between the third movement and finale. In opp. 20 and 33 the tendency is to place the slow movement third where the first moves at a moderate tempo and second where the first movement moves at a faster rate – again in order to obtain maximum tempo contrast. Thereafter Haydn's preference is to place the slow movement second, unless there are particular reasons for placing it third – as in the case of op. 77 no. 2, where the gentle *Andante*, with its long opening duet for first violin and cello, seems ideally placed between the robust and hemiola-filled Minuet and the energetically playful finale. Not only is the slow movement felt to be the centre of gravity in the early quartets (as suggested above), but also in many of the later works, particularly in respect of expression, the profundity and intensity of which, especially from op. 64 onwards, are unforgettable.

TABLE 2
Positioning of slow movements

Movement No.	Total No.	Approximate %
Second	33	49 %
Third	29	43%
First	3	4%
First and third	2	3%
Second and fourth	1	1%

KEYS OF SLOW MOVEMENTS

Choice of key is another significant aspect which is by no means arbitrary. Since the (internal) slow movement of a Haydn quartet is the only one in a different key from that of the first movement, an analysis of the keys of the slow movements (as shown in Table 3 below) provides some interesting statistics.

TABLE 3
Keys of slow movements

Key	Number	Approximate %
Subdominant	29	40.5 %
Dominant	12	17 %
Tonic minor	9	12.5 %
Tonic	5	7 %
Tonic major	5	7 %
Relative major	3	4%
Submediant	2	3 %
Submediant major	1	1.5 %
Flat submediant	1	1.5 %
Sharp submediant	1	1.5 %
Enharmonic flat submediant	1	1.5 %
Mediant major	1	1.5 %
Relative minor	1	1.5 %
TOTAL	71	

The choice of subdominant and dominant for the slow movements (examples of which can be found from the earliest quartets up to and including opp. 74 and 76) is unremarkable, since these were the most usual during the classical era – particularly the subdominant which provides a suitable lowering of tonal tension for this movement. However, in those instances where Haydn moves to *extreme sharp-side* tonalities for his slow movements (the earliest example being op. 64 no. 2, the slow movement of which is in the tonic major, B major, with a key signature one sharp in excess of the normal classical limit of four sharps), the effect is both remarkable and moving. The most extreme example is op. 76 no. 5 in D with its slow movement in F sharp major (with two sharps beyond the normal limit, one of the few other examples of this key signature from the classical era being the Minuet and concluding passage of Haydn's Symphony no. 45). In op. 76 no. 5 Haydn seems intent upon highlighting the tonal contrast between the first and second movements by means of the D major arpeggio at the end of the first movement and F sharp major arpeggio at the beginning of the second.

Equally moving is the E major slow movement of op. 74 no. 3. E major in a slow tempo probably held expressive associations for certain classical composers, most notably Mozart, for whom the key seems to have been reserved mainly for especially sublime moments of emotional, spiritual or natural calm, particularly after a period of turmoil – compare the opening of Fiordiligi's aria in Act II of *Così fan tutte*, or Sarastro's aria in Act II of *Zauberflöte*, or the Act I trio in *Così fan tutte*). Perhaps Haydn was expressing similar feelings in op. 74 no. 3, where the slow movement stands out with an especial warmth and glow – particularly in contrast to the unrelated G minor of the first movement. (Interestingly, a similar overarching key relationship of G minor to E major was chosen for Leonora's great *scena* in Beethoven's *Fidelio*, where the emotional progression is similarly from turmoil to calm.)

Haydn provides examples of contrasts in the opposite tonal direction – that is, of *extreme flat-side* modulations *within* movements, as in the D minor slow movement of op. 50 no. 6, which has a central section in D flat (and which ends in D major). On the face of it, the slow movement of the final (unfinished) quartet, op. 103, appears to juxtapose in its two inner sections extreme flat-side and sharp-side tonalities (the tonal scheme is *A*: B flat; *B*: G flat – D flat; *C (=B')*: C sharp minor – G minor; A: B flat) – until we realize that the C sharp minor represents the enharmonic equivalent, and simplified 'spelling', of D flat minor.

The quartets cited above from opp. 74 and 76 are examples of Haydn's interest, especially in the later works generally (for example, Symphony No. 99), in keys a third apart. Table 4 provides examples of this trend in the quartets.

TABLE 4
Examples of slow movements
with keys a third from the tonic

Op.	No.	Date	Key	Key of slow movt.
74	3	1793	G minor	Sharp submediant
76	5	1797	D	Mediant major
76	6	1797	E flat	Enharmonic flat submediant
77	1	1799	G	Flat submediant
77	2	1799	F	Submediant major
103	-	1803	D minor	Submediant

The most extraordinary example is the slow movement of op. 76 no. 6, which is in B major, but without a key signature, B major standing as the enharmonic equivalent of the flat submediant of the first movement's E flat. (A fuller discussion follows below.)

As mentioned above, this kind of harmonic exploration involves key relationships not only *between* movements (as well as between minuets and trios) but also *within* movements. The slow movement of op. 76 no. 5 provides an especially vivid and expressive example of modulations to keys a third apart – that is, from the dominant chord of C sharp major to E major and from E minor to G major. (The key scheme of the entire movement is summarized in Table 5 below.)

TABLE 5
Key scheme of slow movement of op. 76 no. 5

F sharp... C sharp (b. 18)... C sharp: V (b. 40)... E (b. 41)... E minor (b. 45)... G (b. 51)... F sharp minor (b. 55)... F sharp (b. 63)

The final point about key and harmony concerns the use of 'advanced' harmony, particularly in the late quartets. László

Somfai has demonstrated how Haydn's harmonic language, in the quartets in general and the slow movements in particular, extends into the realm of enharmonic relationships so complex as to require Haydn periodically to simplify his notation and to provide occasional open-note 'props' to assist the players.[2]

Experiments and innovations with key and harmony such as the ones described are often associated with Beethoven – compare the String Quartet op. 18 no. 3, the Second Piano Concerto, the 'Waldstein' Sonata, or the Seventh Symphony – but the true innovator was Haydn.

TOPICS AND EXPRESSION

Leonard G. Ratner defines musical 'topics' in the eighteenth-century sense as 'subjects for musical discourse. Topics appear as fully worked out pieces, i.e. *types*, or as figures and progressions within a piece, i.e. *styles*.'[3] An analysis of discernible topic types in the slow movements [see Table 6 below] shows, as expected, aria (or concerto) as Haydn's favourite type, especially in the earlier quartets.

TABLE 6
Examples of topics in the slow movements

Topic	Op.	No.
Aria or concerto	1	0
	1	1
	1	2
	1	4
	1	6
	2	1
	2	2
	2	4
	9	3
	9	4
	9	6
	17	6

[2] László Somfai, 'A Bold Enharmonic Modulatory Model in Joseph Haydn's String Quartets', in *Studies in Eighteenth-Century Music*, ed. H.C. Robbins Landon (London: Allen and Unwin, 1970), pp. 370-381.
[3] Leonard G. Ratner, *Classic Music: Expression, Form, and Style* (New York: Schirmer Books, 1980), p. 9.

	20	6
	33	5
	33	6
	76	2
Scena	9	2
	17	5
	20	2
Siciliano	9	1
	17	1
	20	5
	50	1

Aria style, that is singing style in the leading part (the first violin in the case of the quartets) with subordinate accompanying parts below, is a conventional topic for slow movements of instrumental pieces during the classical period – compare the slow movement of Mozart's early string quartet, K. 170. The eighteenth-century music historian Charles Burney recognized the operatic nature of Haydn's slow movements when he wrote:

> [Haydn's] *adagios* are often sublime in ideas and the harmony in which they are clad, and... they have a more pathetic effect on my feelings than the finest opera air united with the most exquisite poetry.[4]

The twentieth-century analyst Donald Francis Tovey discerned an element of irony lurking beneath some of these aria-style movements when he likened the first violin in the slow movement of op. 1 no. 1 to

> ... a tragedy queen singing an appeal to generations of ancestral Caesars and accompanying with superb gestures her famous display of *Treffsicherheit* in leaping from deep contralto notes to high soprano and back. The other instruments devoutly accompany, in humble throbbing chords, when her tragic majesty has paused for breath.[5]

As suggested by Daniel Hertz,[6] irony, or at least a hint of it,

[4] Percy Scholes (ed), *Dr. Burney's Musical Tours in Europe*, Vol. II (Central Europe and the Netherlands, 1773 and 1775) (London: Oxford University Press, 1959), p. 60.
[5] Donald Francis Tovey, 'Haydn', in *Cobbett's Cyclopedic Survey of Chamber Music* (London: Oxford University Press, 1929), Vol. I, p. 552.
[6] Daniel Hertz, *Haydn, Mozart and the Viennese School* (New York and London: Norton, 1995), p. 251.

is perhaps also present in the *da chiesa* style of the prelude and postlude which frame the aria.

One of the subtlest of the early aria style movements is the sonata-form third movement, in G major, of op. 1 no. 6. [Ex. 1]

Ex. 1 op. 1 no. 6., III, bb. 1-26 [CD 6]

Here the basic sonority of muted first violin with pizzicato accompanying lower parts informs the entire movement, yet Haydn manages to sustain interest and tension from first note to last. The opening melodic line is broken by rests, in imitation of a singer carefully articulating (Italian) syllables. Covering a range of two octaves and a seventh in the opening section, the 'soloist' combines expressions of tenderness with technical agility in the manner of a skilful operatic soprano. Rhythmic variety further enlivens the melodic line, with triplets, demisemiquavers, suspensions and syncopations combing to form elegant roulades. The figuration interacts closely with the structure: note the way in which the soloist's ascending demisemiquaver rush to a high D coincides with the approach to the dominant of the dominant chord (b. 14), which harmony is further emphasized by strong gestures, especially the descending octave leaps in the first violin (bb. 20-22), followed by expressive sensibility in the upward resolving appoggiaturas (bb. 23 and 24). The concluding cadence of the first section is highlighted by Scotch snaps and the main melodic climax of the movement. The development section includes a Haydnesque false reprise (bb. 31-34) before modulating through C major, G minor and back to the tonic G major, whilst the concluding passage of sensibility is given a climactic feel by the simple expedient of octave transposition.

In three works, aria style becomes *scena* topic. In op. 9 no. 2, after an *Adagio* rhapsodic introduction, in which the first violin covers a range of two octaves and a fourth, the first violin 'sings' a *cantabile* line, which includes a varied reprise in the manner of a *da capo* aria and written out cadenza. In op. 17 no. 5, passages of instrumental recitative alternate with arioso, in a similar manner to the slow movement of Haydn's Symphony no. 7. All these examples of instrumental recitative anticipate, of course,

Beethoven's similar use in, for example, the finale of the Ninth Symphony.

Haydn's most extended example of the *scena* topic is found in the extraordinary slow movement of op. 20 no. 2. [CD 7] Suggesting an orchestral introduction, the unison opening is based on crisp dotted rhythms and angular melodic lines which perhaps represent the *Affekt* of cruelty and pride. [Ex. 2]

Ex. 2 op. 20 no. 2, II, bb. 1-4

Although this type of figuration was the common stock of eighteenth and early nineteenth-century composers – compare a similar example in the slow movement of Beethoven's Fourth Piano Concerto – the opening theme is of a highly arresting nature and its transformation, into a soft and tender, even pleading, cello solo accompanied by a throbbing accompaniment which perhaps suggests fear, is remarkable.[7] [Ex. 3]

Ex. 3 Haydn op. 20 no. 2, II, bb. 5-8

[7] I am grateful to my colleague Dr. David Ledbetter for drawing my attention to Anton Raphael Meng's painting, 'Cleopatra Before Octavius', which represents visually some of the expressive themes found in the Haydn movement. Although any such correspondence is obviously coincidental, the similarities point to a common dramatic intent through different mediums.

The second main period is in the style of *arioso*, [Ex. 4] with the first violin acting as *prima donna* (a role taken over briefly by the second violin); although the expression is subdued and the style *cantabile*, the agitated character of the opening is never far from the surface – compare the busy viola accompaniment – and periodically reappears. This movement represents Haydn's most vivid essay in transferring the operatic style to the quartet medium.

In later works a singing style is nearly always felt in the slow movements (and Haydn is rarely given the credit he deserves as a supreme melodist) but he seems to move away from the aria style to a different level – that of deeply expressive song with dense, rich textures in which all the instruments contribute, as if in a hymn of praise, one of the best examples being the slow movement of op. 76 no. 3 (which is, in one sense, literally a hymn of praise in that it is based on The Emperor's Hymn, 'Gott erhalte Franz den Kaiser').

FORM

Binary (particularly in opp. 1 and 2), sonata, through (that is, without internal double bars), and variation forms are found in

Ex. 4 op. 20 no. 2, II, bb. 34-37

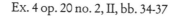

the slow movements. In general, development sections do not figure prominently in the sonata form movements, perhaps partly because of considerations of length. Haydn appears to have turned away by and large from schemes with internal double bars and repeats after op. 33 no. 1, possibly finding this kind of movement too long. A somewhat different approach is represented by op. 50 no. 6, where the passage immediately after the double bar is more like a variation of the main theme than a development of it, with further variations in the recapitulation. The most common type of sonata form is the through-composed type – that is, with vestiges of sonata form tonic-dominant polarity, but without repeats, a fine example of which is the third movement in B flat of op. 33 no. 2. Here the gently opening two-part counterpoint undergoes various textural transformations on its modulatory journey away from and back to the tonic. Equally memorable are op. 50 no. 5 ('The Dream') and op. 76 no. 5.

Variation form is perhaps the most characteristic and interesting of Haydn's structures. In fact, variation technique plays a part in most of his music, as exact repetition often seemed to be anathema to him. However, in the more limited sense, the variation slow movements (which form about a third of the total) can be categorised as shown in Table 7.

TABLE 7
Categories of Variation Form with examples

Type of Variation Form	Op.	No.
Single theme	2	6
	9	5, I
	20	4
	20	5
	50	1
	54	2
	55	3
	64	1
	64	2
	64	3
	64	4
	64	5
	64	6
	71	1
	71	2
	74	2
	74	3
	76	2
	76	3
	77	2
Double theme	55	2
	71	3
	76	1
	103	
Rondo	50	3
	54	3

One of the most graceful examples of 'single-theme' variation form is provided by the slow movement of op. 20 no. 4. Here the minor mode theme, marked *Un poco adagio e affetuoso*, is informed by a quality of courtly sophistication and affectation as revealed by an ostensibly sorrowful melodic line, the affectation of which is perhaps betrayed by jaunty dotted rhythms on the approach to cadence points. The climactic ascent in the second half is enhanced by sophisticated part writing and carefully placed diminished and augmented sixths chords. [Ex. 5]

Ex. 5 op. 20 no. 4, II, bb. 1-18 [CD 8]

Here we have perhaps another example of that quality of irony which lurks behind a few of the slow movements. The ensuing variations feature different instruments in turn, after which the theme returns in its original form, followed by an extended coda which becomes increasingly operatic, even *scena*-like, in expression. How doubly ironic that such courtly sophistication should be followed by a gypsy dance – that is, the *Menuetto: Allegretto alla Zingarese*.

The slow movements of op. 20 no. 5 and op. 54 no. 2 (and, to a lesser degree, op. 50 no. 1) are similar to each other in that the theme is heard initially in full, sonorous, four-part harmony and is then transferred to the lower three instruments whilst the first violin weaves a series of quasi-improvisational roulades above. In op. 20 no. 5 a graceful *siciliano* style informs the whole movement. In op. 54 no. 2 the style is quite different. [CD 9] Here the C minor mode and low tessitura give to the theme a singularly sombre quality. The theme is then repeated three times in the tonic, apart from the second repetition which begins in the relative major. Displaying an astonishing degree of rhythmic and harmonic freedom the like of which was probably not to be encountered again in the string quartet until the time of Bartók, the first violin weaves its roulades perhaps in imitation of an improvising gypsy violinist. [Ex. 6]

Ex. 6 op. 54 no. 2, II, bb. 1-18

The E flat slow movement of op. 50 no. 1 represents another kind of variation form, of which Haydn was to become especially fond – that is, variations with a central section in the minor mode in order to obtain maximum expressive contrast. The basic scheme is: $A - A^I - B (=A^{II}) - A^{III}$, within which the B section is in the tonic minor. The scheme is simplified somewhat in four of the op. 64 set (nos. 3-6) to $A - B - A^I$.

In op. 64 no. 5, [CD 10] the opening theme is harmonised with full, rich sonorities, [Ex. 7] the brief minor key passage towards the end of which (bb. 17-22) not only further intensifies the expression but anticipates the key of the B section (bb. 35 ff.), which is itself a variation of the opening theme.

Ex. 7 op. 64 no. 5, II, bb. 1-41

The use of the tonic minor mode and its relative major at this point (bb. 35 ff.) enables Haydn to exploit the very bottom of the cello's register and thereby produce perhaps the richest texture in the entire movement: a kind of textural climax. Characteristically, the variations in the return of the *A* section are carried out primarily in the first violin, which weaves a rich array of roulades made up of figures such as the *ribattuta* (rapid alternations of lower or upper auxiliaries, as at b. 55), *tirata* (or scale, in b. 56), and *retardatio* (or syncopations against changes of harmony, in b. 57), the cumulative effect of which is expressive intensification at the highest artistic level.[8] [Ex. 8]

Ex. 8 op. 64 no. 5, II, bb. 51-8

[8] See Ratner, *op. cit.*, pp. 83-85 for a sample of this "rich vocabulary of melodic figures [which was] codified and labelled in dictionaries, manuals, and lexicons".

Headed by the slowest tempo in Haydn's entire quartet oeuvre – *Largo assai* (although the actual tempo is somewhat moderated by the metre of two minims per bar) – the slow movement of op. 74 no. 3 [Ex. 9 and CD 11] follows a similar structure to the op. 64 examples (*A – B – A'*).

Ex. 9 op. 74 no. 3, II, bb. 1-37

Especially rich in texture, the *A* section reaches an expressive climax before the first double bar, as the first violin peaks on an octave B, with the other parts combining to form a German sixth chord, the climactic feature of which is reinforced by double stopping in all instruments except the second violin, which has instead an octave leap on E sharp. The reason for the relatively low tessitura of the opening phrase becomes apparent at b. 15, where the phrase is repeated, to ethereal effect, an octave higher. Section *B*, in the tonic minor, is a variation on the opening melodic line and, like the *A* section, reaches a textural and harmonic climax by means of a German sixth chord. The following duet between the two outer instruments, accompanied by throbbing inner parts which periodically close in with piquant dissonances, expresses restraint and intensity by turns. Amongst the varied figurations in the return of the *A* section two bars stand out for their breathtaking effect. The Neapolitan harmony of bb. 12 and 13 is here reproduced, again [*subito*] *pianissimo*, but now in a *tremolando* version which looks forward to Schubert's G major Quartet, op. 161.

The earliest example of double-theme variation form in the slow movements of the quartets is found in op. 55 no. 2 (although earlier examples can be found in other genres, such as in Symphony no. 70). The two themes, which are clearly related – the first in the minor, the second in the tonic major [Ex. 10 and 11] – are each subjected to two variations which were probably designed to provide a showcase for Johann Tost,[9] although as

Ex. 10 op. 55 no. 2, I, bb. 1-8

[9] Compare Denis McCaldin's discussion (pp. 46-7) of the violinist Johann Tost (Ed.).

Ex. 11 op. 55 no. 2, I, bb. 27-35 (first section of second theme)

the variations progress, the other parts become increasingly involved, especially in the final variation, where the cello, in the
treble clef, holds the second theme for an extended period. In
short, double theme variation form was an innovation of Haydn's, of which he was to become increasingly fond (and which
was destined to have such a powerful influence on Beethoven,
most notably in the slow movement of the Ninth Symphony).

As mentioned above, op. 76 no. 6 contains perhaps the most
remarkable slow movement of all. [Ex. 12] Without opening key
signature, the movement is notated in B major, which represents
the enharmonic flattened submediant (C flat major) of the first
movement's E flat.

Ex. 12 op. 76 no. 6, II, bb. 1-39 [CD 12]

Statements of the sublime theme are separated by solo scalic passages which lead into increasingly fantastic tonal areas: not for
nothing is the movement labelled 'Fantasia'. For example, the
first transposed statement of the theme begins in E major, and
moves through E minor before cadencing in G; the next statement modulates from B flat major through B flat minor to B
major as the enharmonic equivalent of C flat major. Passing
through further fantastic modulations, the theme gradually makes
its way back to B major (or C flat!), this time with the five-sharp
key signature installed, at which point Haydn provides the most
extended contrapuntal passage in the movement.[10] The most remarkable aspect of all is the way in which such complexity is
concealed: the listener can be profoundly moved by the movement's intense lyricism whilst remaining blissfully ignorant of
its complex harmonic structure. In short, variation technique
here is concerned less with thematic or rhythmic variation, more
with harmonic and contrapuntal exploration.

CONCLUSION

The degree of invention and innovation in the slow movements never ceases to astonish. In terms of variety of number,
order and, in particular, positioning of movements, as well as
choice of keys both between and within movements, Haydn's
range is vast. Binary, sonata, through-composed, and variations
constitute his armoury of structures; aria, concerto, *scena*, and
siciliano, his main topics. Expression ranges from the objective
and occasionally ironic to the intensely profound. Some of the
harmonic experiments are, in terms of (concealed) intellectual
complexity, amongst the boldest of the classical era. Above all,
Haydn succeeds in touching our deepest feelings.

[10] A full harmonic analysis is provided by Somfai, *op. cit.*, pp. 375-377.

IV

Minuets and Trios in Haydn's Quartets

David Wyn Jones

INTRODUCTION

First impressions might encourage the listener and the unwary player to regard minuets in Haydn's quartets as the slightest movement in the typical cycle of four, lacking the sustained intellectual enterprise of sonata movements or the engaging lyricism and gentle pathos of slow movements. They are certainly the shortest movement in the quartet, but they should not be regarded as a mere interlude, a pleasant interruption to the more serious business of the rest of the quartet. Within a compact time limit and the standard broad framework of minuet, trio and repeat of the minuet, they reveal a creative imagination that is as distinctive as that found in other movements. Indeed, they have a precision and a concision of expression that is found nowhere else in the cycle; very few notes are wasted and Haydn's abilities as a miniaturist in music deserve to be as celebrated as much as his mastery of broader canvases.

Like many of his contemporaries in Austria, Haydn wrote minuets for actual dancing, where the requirements of patterned physical movement dictated that the music should flow evenly and without disruption: a series of regular four-bar phrases, no cross-accentuation, a marked emphasis (particularly in the bass) on crotchet rhythms and a homophonic texture. While such minuets are attractive enough as functional dance music, they could not be imported wholesale into the quartet. They would have lacked the imagination of the surrounding movements, particularly in the way that they did not exploit any interplay between the four players; they would then, indeed, have sounded like interludes. It is no accident that there is no instance in Haydn's quartets – or, for that matter, his symphonies, sonatas and trios – of minuets already written for dances being incorporated into a work.

Nevertheless, appreciation of this dance background is vital for any sensitive performance of Haydn's minuets in his instrumental music, since they are often composed as gentle distor-

tions of the minuet, sometimes fulfilling expectations of the
dance, sometimes thwarting or undermining them, and, of course,
always exploiting the medium of four inquisitive players. Living
in a pervasive dance culture that included the minuet, it was
certainly much easier for Haydn's players and listeners to appreciate this intriguing tussle between form and content than it is
for modern players and listeners. But with a little conscious ef-
fort, it is perfectly possible to regain the thought processes of
eighteenth-century musicians and audiences. We will take three
minuets from quartets by Haydn, from three different periods
in his life – the late 1750s, the early 1780s and the late 1790s –
and probe this relationship between the minuet as a dance and
the minuet as a studied composition.

Op. 1 No. 1 in B flat ('La Chasse')

This quartet is one of ten written by Haydn between c. 1757
and 1762. It was later published as op. 1 no. 1, but it is certainly
not Haydn's first work in any genre and almost certainly not
the first of these ten early quartets to be composed. All ten quartets have five movements with two minuets. The fourth movement of op. 1 no. 1 is a particularly interesting example. [Ex. 1]

Ex. 1 op. 1 no. 1, IV, second Minuet [CD 13]

There are many features here that are taken from the dance: the obvious binary structure, the continual emphasis on the steady tread of crotchets and, if one were to focus on the top of the texture, most of the phrases are four-bar phrases. But throughout the Minuet, and with increasing determination, Haydn undermines the regularity of the phrasing patterns. The process starts in the very first phrase when the viola and cello imitate the two violins at the distance of a bar, whereas in a dance minuet they would have typically offered homophonic support from the beginning. The end result is a four-bar phrase with two beginnings. The violins continue with a four-bar phrase but at the point of closure, the viola and cello initiate a new beginning to the phrase; the violins continue with another four-bar phrase (bb. 9-12) but, once again, the viola and cello undermine the pattern with a would-be beginning. In this opening section, therefore, whereas the two violins proceed with an impeccable series of three four-bar phrase, the viola and cello do their best to mask this regularity by either entering late or early.

Much of the energy of this beginning is due to the raw scoring: violins in octaves, and the disruptive viola and cello also in octaves. Many minuets in Haydn's early quartets have this octave scoring, a sonority that caused a good deal of criticism in more conservative areas of Europe. For instance, a commentator in Hamburg wrote:

Haydn is pleasant, witty and full of inventiveness in his quartets; his symphonies and trios are of the same mettle. Whether, however, his minuets in octaves are to everyone's taste is something I will leave undecided. They are good for amusement; but one easily gets the idea that one is hearing father and son begging by singing octaves; and that is a bad object for musical imitation.[1]

The beggars become more unruly after the double bar, with the second violin contradicting the first, and the viola and cello contradicting the second violin. The thematic material itself is clearly derived from the main theme and the tonality changes to the tonic minor; it is a miniature development, as often in Haydn's instrumental minuets. After the half-close into b. 18, it would be reasonable to expect a return of the main theme to complete the structure. Haydn, however, avoids this routine pattern and instead intensifies the process of phrase beginnings being contradicted. Bars 19-26 happen to form a segment of eight bars but there is no feeling of four plus four as one pair of beggars (viola and cello) vie with the second pair (first and second violins) to establish the real beginning of a phrase. This masterly control of language and medium is a remarkable tribute to Haydn's inventiveness, even in this apparently apprentice period of his life.

If we now turn to the Trio we see (and hear) that it offers a complete contrast. Here is music that could be danced to: sixteen bars divided into a series of regular four-bar phrases; emphasis on crotchet beats; and all four players accentuating with a *forte* the beginning of each phrase. With no disruption whatsoever, the Trio acts as a perfect foil for the surrounding Minuet, a common expressive ploy in Haydn minuets and trios. [Ex. 2]

Ex. 2 op. 1 no. 1, IV, Trio of second Minuet

[1] Quoted in H.C. Robbins Landon, *Haydn: Chronicle and Works. Haydn at Eszterháza 1766-1790* (London: Thames and Hudson, 1978), p. 132.

Minuet da capo

OP. 33 NO. 2 IN E FLAT

In 1781, Haydn completed six quartets that were published the following year in Vienna. Before their publication by the firm of Artaria, Haydn offered manuscript copies to certain selected patrons. Three letters offering these manuscript copies survive – probably many more were written – and all describe the six quartets as being written "in a new and special way" ("auf eine ganz neue besondere Art").[2] To a certain extent, this was sales talk designed to encourage purchasers, but there are many 'new' features too. Instead of minuets and trios, all six quartets have movements that are labelled 'Scherzo' and, for the section conventionally labelled the trio, no title. These are the first quartets by Haydn to use the label Scherzo, but they are not the one-in-a-bar fast movement familiar from the nineteenth century, and, in truth, they could easily have been labelled minuets and trios. The word 'scherzo' literally means a jest, but while these movements are certainly witty, humorous and whimsical, they are no more so than other minuets and trios by the composer. After op. 33, Haydn reverted to the normal title of Minuet and Trio,

---

[2] Compare Denis McCaldin's discussion (pp. 43 ff.) of the "new and special way" in which those quartets were composed (Ed.).

even for those movements that are close to the nineteenth-century one-in-a-bar Scherzo. The title is so closely associated with op. 33 that the set as a whole is sometimes referred to as '*Gli Scherzi*'.

Op. 33 no. 2 is probably the most humorous of the six scherzos in the set, cleverly whimsical in the Scherzo itself, outrageously vulgar in the Trio section. Let us deal with the Scherzo first. [Ex. 3]

Ex. 3 op. 33 no. 2, II, Scherzo [CD 14]

Even more than in the Minuet in op. 1 no. 1, the rhythmic patterns of this movement emphasize the beat. This type of emphasis, which in an actual dance might have been accompanied by an exaggerated stamping of the feet, was a feature of the contemporary Deutsche, a variant of the minuet. Mozart in the Minuet of Symphony no. 39 (K.543) evokes the same stamping quality with even greater aplomb. But, again, it is the denial of a full danced Deutsche that makes Haydn's example so intriguing. The first unexpected event is the echo phrase in bb. 5-6, which as well as being in a softer dynamic has a niggling appoggiatura C flat added to the dominant harmony, and – this joke is for the players – has the second violin playing above the first violin.

After the double bar, Haydn takes the quaver figure that had led to the previous cadence and uses it in imitation between first and second violin. Following the close at b. 20, Haydn could easily have begun the reprise of the main melody. Instead, he interpolates a passage based on the previous *piano* interruption, delaying the reprise until b. 23. The actual reprise is then a literal one. The paradox of the movement is that the material itself implies a foot-stomping dance, but the interpolations, in particular, ensure something more reserved. In fact, by simply omitting the *piano* interpolations in bb. 5-6 and bb. 21-5 and slightly adjusting the quaver passages in bb. 17-18, it is quite easy to convert the music back into its implied model, a movement suitable for dancing. [Ex. 4 overleaf]

The Trio section, as in the Minuet from op. 1 no. 1, provides a contrast, one that in a way fulfils the desire of the Scherzo itself to become something more vulgar. [Ex. 5 overleaf and CD 15]

Ex. 4 op. 33 no. 2, II, Scherzo – recomposed version by DWJ

Ex. 5 op. 33 no. 2, II, Trio (Edition Peters)

Edition Peters

D.C. al Fine.

The music is in a uniform dynamic throughout; it is led by the first violin with the other three instruments providing a simple and repetitive accompaniment, and there are no interruptions to the easy and continuing series of four-bar phrases. The accompaniment, in particular, comes very close to the style of Austrian folk music, such as is today typically encountered in the *Schuhplattler* evenings inflicted on drunken parties of British skiers. Very little documentary evidence survives from before the early nineteenth century on Austrian folk music, but there is little doubt that Haydn was evoking the eighteenth-century precursor of *Schuhplattler* music. The clinching evidence would seem to be that until comparatively recently, all editions of this music ignored Haydn's careful markings in the first violin part, all designed to suggest a folk idiom. The indicated fingering as well as the indications *'sull'istessa corda'* and the wavy line all produce *glissandi*. By simply omitting these markings, nineteenth-century editors changed this picture of a one-finger peasant violinist slithering around the music to something more decorous. It is particularly audacious, even for Haydn. [Ex. 6 and CD 16]

Ex. 6 op. 33 no. 2, II, Trio (Doblinger edition, with slides in first violin)

Da Capo fin al Segno 𝄌

Op. 77 No. 2 in F

Op. 77 no. 2 was Haydn's last completed quartet, composed in 1799 and published together with a quartet in G major as a pair in 1802. He had hoped to complete the standard set of six works but only two movements – a minuet and a slow movement – were completed of a third quartet, in D minor; this unfinished work was published in 1806 and later became known as op. 103.

Headed *Menuet: Presto*, the Minuet from op. 77 no. 2 [Ex. 7 and CD 17] is a very brisk movement, clearly one-in-a-bar rather than the three-in-a-bar of the Minuet from op. 1 no. 1 and the Scherzo from op. 33 no. 2.

Ex. 7 op. 77 no. 2, II, Minuet

Together with the Minuets of op. 76 no. 1 and op. 77 no. 1, it is one of three quartets by Haydn from the late 1790s with this designation. In tempo and spirit, they are recognisably scherzos but, whereas Beethoven – in works such as the piano sonatas op. 2, the string trios op. 9 and the quartets op. 18 – used the word scherzo, Haydn preferred to use the traditional word minuet, but to qualify it with the fast tempo marking. Given

the traditional image of the minuet as a stately dance, one might
be tempted to think that these *presto* minuets were contradic-
tions in terms, and that Haydn was simply using the traditional
term for this kind of movement without any implication that it
related to a familiar dance form. But there is ample evidence to
suggest that there were two distinct minuet traditions in Vienna
at the turn of the century, the traditional stately minuet and the
much faster one-in-a-bar minuet. The Minuet in Haydn's unfinished quartet in D minor (op. 103) suggests that players were
familiar with these very fast minuets; it is headed '*Menuetto ma
non troppo Presto*'.

But as always in Haydn's quartets, this *presto* Minuet defies
social dancing. Here, it is not imitation or interpolated phrase
lengths that principally undermine the required regularity, but
the propensity of the material to mix subdivisions of the beat
that are felt in threes with those that suggest twos. The opening
four bars show this mix immediately. The second violin, viola
and cello have the standard division into threes, while the first
violin line could easily have been written in 2/4 against these
threes. The following phrase is initiated by a bouncing, staccato
figure in the cello which can be played both ways: in a pattern
that emphasizes the lower note, a duple division of the beat, or,
more consciously, one that pushes the figure into a triple division of the beat. This metric unease pervades the entire Minuet;
only the two pause bars (bb. 43-4) that herald the reprise of the
main theme do not feature this conflict. Such a conflict was fundamental to the later dance known as the Furiant, examples of
which abound in Dvořák's music. In Haydn's case, it is one of
the most carefully controlled and crafted movements in his entire output; that it is also easy to listen to (but certainly not to
play) is very much part of Haydn's distinctive outlook on composition.

Unusually, Haydn indicates a bar's rest between the Minuet
and Trio, suggesting a break but at the same a sense of continuity between the two. The most ear-catching feature of the Trio
is its key, D flat major, a rich and sonorous contrast. Increasingly in the 1790s, Haydn had shown an interest in placing trio
sections (slow movements too) in keys that are a third away from
the tonic, rather than the more conventional fourth, fifth or

change of mode.[3] Its prime purpose here is one of colour, but it supports a musical texture that could not be more different from that of the Minuet. The one-in-a-bar pulse subdivides easily and continuously into threes; the dynamic is *pianissimo*; the music is *legato* rather than staccato; and sustained tonic pedal points underpin much of the texture. Having controlled the move from Minuet to Trio, Haydn does the same thing from the Trio back into the Minuet by having a nine-bar link that hesitantly anticipates the thematic material of the Minuet and moves the tonality from D flat to F. [Ex. 8]

Ex. 8 op. 77 no. 2, II, Trio

---

[3] Compare David Young's discussion (pp. 61-2) of key relationships a third apart in the slow movements (Ed.).

Menuet da capo ma forte

CONCLUSION

Haydn was once asked his view about an intriguing aspect of music pedagogy, the use of the interval of the fourth in the so-called 'Palestrina style'. Haydn's reply showed that he was more interested in modern composition than pedagogy.

> Art is free, and will be limited by no pedestrian rules. The ear, assuming it is trained, must decide, and I consider myself as competent as any to legislate here. Such affectations are worthless; I would rather someone tried to compose a really *new* minuet.[4]

[4] V. Gotwals (ed.), *Haydn: Two Contemporary Portraits* (Wisconsin: University of Wisconsin Press, 1963), p. 61.

Haydn had been fascinated by minuet composition all his life and had written several hundred examples, with those in his quartets, in particular, revealing the sense of newness in a particularly inventive way. Two hundred years later, this fascination that Haydn clearly felt is still undervalued, by performers and commentators alike.

V

Haydn's Quartet Finales and Cyclical Closure

Michael Spitzer

INTRODUCTION

What makes a final movement a *finale*? Haydn's very last string quartet, op. 103 in D minor, was left unfinished at his death as a two-movement torso. Its final movement is a haunting Trio in D major which is suffused with the valedictory resignation one associates more with the late Beethoven.[1] Although, technically, the *da capo* of the Minuet has the last word, is it permissible to regard Haydn's Trio as a 'finale', and, if not, why? Is a movement a 'finale' purely by virtue of its end-position in a string quartet, or do some other factors come into play? The two chief factors are convention and context. To understand the quartets is to hear them against a background of conventional procedures, one of which is that a trio is a middle movement. Listening to a finale *contextually*, on the other hand, means to grasp the way it provides the entire quartet with its sense of an ending (endings determine, and are determined by, the meaning of the whole story). Although each of the four (or five) movements of a quartet needs to be understood in the context of the work's overall shape and content, this seems to be particularly true of the finale. For this reason, my discussion of Haydn's finales will necessarily go beyond the bounds of the movements immediately at hand.

HOW FINALES RESOLVE

Haydn was the first composer to fully grasp how a finale can define the global structure of a string quartet. By virtue of its end position, a finale can frame, fulfil, bind together and conclude a work: in short, it affords it closure. More than any other movement, the finale has obligations beyond itself, and it is in

---

[1] See Beethoven's own final quartet, op. 135 in F.

the finale that Haydn's drive towards cyclical unity is most clearly expressed.[2] A chronological survey of the quartets therefore tells us as much about the evolution of the finale genre as about Haydn's attitude to large-scale formal closure. The present study explores these interlinked questions through five quartets spanning Haydn's entire career: op. 1 no. 1 in B flat (1763); op. 20 no. 2 in C (1772); op. 33 no. 5 in G (1781); op. 54 no. 2 in C (1788); op. 76 no. 3 in C (1796). These five quartets achieve closure in their finales in very different ways. We gain a measure of their individuality, however, by considering them in relation to some common principles.

Music theory has long known that closure involves much more than a mere return to the tonic; rather, it emerges from a complex of interacting rhythmic, harmonic, and thematic processes.[3] The higher up we go in the pyramid of form (with phrases at the bottom and the whole piece at the top), the messier this interaction becomes. The issues here are far too complex to address in a single chapter. Nevertheless, for the purpose of clarity, it might be helpful to sketch out some basic strategies operative in the quartets. The finales of Haydn's quartets afford closure according to four 'models':

1) *Symmetrical Model*

The finale balances the first movement. The notion of 'balance' predicates an architectural concept of music as a series of 'blocks' in space. Alternatively, it suggests the principles of poetic rhyme, whereby the movements chime with each other. Either way, it projects onto the global level the quintessential Classical principles of symmetry and equilibrium, which are normally discussed on the lower levels of phrasing and section. The outer movements are 'in balance' when their duration, weighting, and material more or less correspond.

2) *Linear Model*

The finale constitutes a goal. The Linear Model reminds us that

---

[2] The issue of cyclic form in Haydn has been brought to the forefront of debate by James Webster's *Haydn's Farewell Symphony and the Idea of Classical Style: Through-Composition and Cyclic Integration in his Instrumental Music* (Cambridge: Cambridge University Press, 1991).
[3] For a broad discussion of Haydn's techniques of closure, see my 'The Retransition as Sign: Listener-Orientated Approaches to Tonal Closure in Haydn's Sonata-Form Movements', *Journal of the RMA* 121 (1996), pp. 11-45.

musical 'form' in fact unfolds through time, in a forward motion. From this perspective, the finale behaves like a glorified cadence. Just as lower levels of the Classical style are functionally differentiated according to a 'beginning-middle-end' pattern, the Linear Model stresses the contrast, rather than the balance, of the outer movements.

3) *Process Model*
The finale resumes and completes 'unfinished business'. Another aspect of Classical music is that it argues. The material presented at the opening typically provides topics for discussion amongst the four individuals who perform the quartet; the basis for a developmental process. Like the Linear Model, the Process Model foregrounds music's temporal aspect. But the stress is now on the particularity of the material, rather than on normative functional progressions. For example, the finale can 'resolve' motivic or tonal issues active throughout the work.

4) *Commentary Model*
The finale parodies or reinterprets previous material. This is the most subtle yet far-reaching of the four models, since it embraces the nature of the entire musical discourse.

These four models are not mutually exclusive; they operate simultaneously in different strengths. Moreover, they are realised within five 'frames':

1) *Motivic Frame* – thematic ideas or pitch cells;
2) *Topical Frame* – textural and tonal categories;
3) *Formal Frame* – conventional formal patterns;
4) *Genre Frame* – conventional genre types;
5) *Aesthetic Frame* – intellectual and stylistic paradigms.

The list suggests an increase in sophistication from Frame 1 to 5. Although, like the four models, all five frames can coexist in the same piece, there is a compelling sense that the progression maps onto the evolution of Haydn's style from op. 1 to op. 76. Unity in op. 1 largely involves correspondences between miniature ideas; op. 76, by contrast, unfolds a broader narrative of 'darkness' yielding to 'light'. By codifying Haydn's procedure in this way, we can track the changes in his style without needing to show that it also gets 'better'. Haydn's first quartet was the work of a mature composer in his thirties, and it is the premise of this chapter that the same intellectual underpinnings which support the later quartets were already in place in 1763.

OP. 1 NO. 1 IN B FLAT

Haydn's first quartet follows the five-movement arrangement typical of his divertimenti: a central *Adagio* framed on either side by two *Menuetto*s and two *Prestos*. The finale closes the quartet primarily on grounds of balance, given that it returns to the tempo character (*presto*) and form (sonata) of the first movement. Stylistically, it is very much of its time. [CD 18]

Its miniature proportions display the origins of sonata form in the rounded binary dance, with a twenty-seven-bar exposition and a development of only fourteen bars which is little more than a decorated dominant pedal. The texture is dominated by the first violin, with the cello frequently reduced to repeated quavers. The fabric of the music comprises a mosaic of stereotypical *galant* harmonic and motivic patterns. What Haydn does with this simple and conventional material is as sophisticated as one would expect.

Take the triplet semiquaver turn of bar 1 (G-F-E flat-D) – a favourite *galant* cliché. Not only does the turn permeate the surface of the piece (the standard index of motivic coherence), but it is projected into the harmonic middleground. Haydn builds his transition section (bb. 7-13) by transposing the scale to the dominant (D-C-Bb-A), augmenting each step into a full bar, and passing it in dialogue between the violins. [Ex 1]

Ex. 1 op. 1 no. 1, V, bb. 1-17

Ornament is thus transformed into structure. A common technique, *circa* 1770, of modulating from I to V was to end the tonic group on scale-step $\hat{3}$, and then convert $\hat{3}$ to $\hat{6}$ of the new key, which is arrived at via a $\hat{6}$-$\hat{5}$-$\hat{4}$-$\hat{3}$ descent. Though prevalent in the op. 9 quartets of 1769, this device is rare in op. 1.[4] Its presence in this movement is surely motivated (pun intended) by the ornament in bar 1.

According to our Model 2, the *Presto* constitutes not only a rhyme with the first movement but a goal. If we strip away the diminutions in the opening two bars, we get a descending fanfare F-D-Bb, a reversal of the rising fanfare which opens the quartet, and which gave it its nickname of 'The Hunt'. If the quartet begins with an opening gambit, it concludes with an 'end sign' (descents conventionally signal endings). A similar reversal obtains between the development sections of the outer movements. Bars 28-39 of the finale trace an alternation of two ideas: the turn figure in the second violin and viola is answered by a semiquaver flourish in the first violin. [Ex. 2 overleaf] This inverts the order originally presented at bb. 24-28 of the first movement, with the first violin semiquaver flourish answered by a turn figure in

---

[4] See, for example, the outer movements of op. 9 no. 2: first movement bb. 15-19; fourth movement bb. 7-10.

Ex. 2 op. 1 no. 1, V, bb. 28-44

quavers. [Ex. 3] Note also how the quaver turn in the first *Presto* at bb. 25-26 and bb. 27-28 foreshadows the outline of the first violin in the second *Presto*, C-D-E flat-D-C.

Ex. 3 op. 1 no. 1, I, bb. 25-28

Despite the neutrality of Haydn's material, he deploys it with maximum transparency, so as to foster recognition. While the turn is consigned to the margins (the development) of *Presto* 1, it is lifted to centre stage (the first subject) in *Presto* 2. In line with Model 3, the finale thus prosecutes and resolves unfinished business. Finally, with Model 4, the finale reinterprets the order of events in the first movement. It effects a role-reversal, whereby a marginal ornament is brought forward to the first bar of the piece, and then embedded within the guts of the harmonic structure. The 'story' of op. 1 no. 1 is the reconciliation of a *galant* decorative aesthetic with a new, organic, perspective on musical structure.

Op. 20 No. 2 in C

Haydn's 'Sun' quartets evince an unprecedented breadth of conception. Haydn expands his tonal framework, and fortifies his texture with contrapuntal techniques. The latter is manifest in the more equal interaction of the four voices, as well as in the three celebrated fugal finales, of which this is the first. It might at first seem that Haydn's recourse to fugal texture represents a relapse to a more conservative style; an easy short-cut to a continuity of argument which had eluded him in previous finales. Nevertheless, just as with the *galant* clichés, it is what Haydn *does* with these contrapuntal techniques which marks him out as progressive. Paradoxically, the stylistic jolt from the *Menuetto* to the *Fuga* provides the finale with just the 'kick' it needs in order to function as the climax of the entire quartet. [CD 19] The work thus represents a thoroughly *progressive* tendency to give the finale a specific gravity equal to that of the first movement, or even, as in this case, of making it the quartet's goal (Model 2). The fugal finales of Beethoven's 'Hammerklavier' Sonata and B flat Quartet op. 130 are inconceivable without Haydn's example. A further novelty of Haydn's fugue is its evolutionary progress: after a severely contrapuntal exposition, the Baroque style is overtaken by episodic passage-work in an up-to-date *galant* style. It is as if Haydn conflates two axes of temporality: the 'performance time' of musical development, and the 'historical time' of the development of style. Beethoven's fugues also do this but, once again, 'Haydn the Innovator' got there first.

What makes this fugue *classical* is, very simply, the nature of the relationship between the opening and the overall form. As we shall see, Haydn is interested as much in the overall shape of the fugal exposition as in the potential of its constituent themes.

The *Fuga a 4 Soggetti* begins strictly, with the principal subject introduced by the first violin and passed down, respectively, to second violin, viola, and cello. [Ex. 4]

Ex. 4 op. 20 no. 2, IV, bb. 1-15

The subject is joined by three countersubjects: a syncopated descending scale in the viola, b. 2; a rising scale idea, again in the viola, b. 5; a semiquaver figure in the first violin at b. 12, shadowing the rising scale idea (now in the viola) in parallel thirds. Apparent beneath the skin of this otherwise conventional routine, however, is a strikingly bold design. The four subjects divide into two complementary pairs of themes, one pair falling, chromatic and syncopated (subjects 1 and 2), the other rising, diatonic, and metrically regular (subjects 3 and 4). This order of exposition is reflected in the general course of the fugue, whereby themes 3 and 4 gradually take over and eclipse the principal pair. Listen to the *galant* homophonic textures which end the piece.

A more profound process turns on the very identity of the first subject. It is a truism of fugue that subjects are constantly reinterpreted by their changing contrapuntal context. The present fugue explores the ambiguities of its opening octave leap. When Haydn's initial subject is heard unaccompanied, as at b. 1, the lower G of this leap continues to sound, rather like an implicit dominant pedal, undercutting the subject's V-I resolution to C in b. 2, and connecting registrally with the viola's F (and its successive steps E, D and C). When the subject is assumed by the second violin at b. 4, it is given new harmonic support by the third subject in the viola. The viola's rising scale from C to F realises the first subject's implied fifth progression. It is important that this stabilisation happens on the tonic (I) and on a lower instrument, since it suggests an overall drift from dominant pedal to tonic, from high instrument to low. Indeed, the final entry of the first subject (b. 11) is a tonic statement on the cello. Although the arrangement of these entries is perfectly normal from a Baroque viewpoint, Haydn's conceit lies in projecting its underlying 'drift towards stabilisation' across the entire movement. The long-deferred tonic reprise of the first subject, at b. 151, emerges from a now-realised dominant pedal, and is resolved by the bottom C of bar 156. [Ex. 5] The special sonority of this open-string C natural in the cello clinches the global resolution of the finale.[5] If the 'story' of the exposition had been the search of a violin's dominant pedal for a solid cello tonic, then the narrative reaches its triumphant culmination here. Although all four subjects are recapitulated at b. 151, they are subsumed within this expansive G-C cadential gesture, whose dynamics are decidedly un-Baroque: the music has 'grown up'.

Ex. 5 op. 20 no. 2, IV, bb. 150-162

The finale's unstintingly teleological design overrides its formal anomalies. As William Drabkin has observed in the most recent study of this piece, the fugal statements are not set off from the episodes very clearly.[6] At comparable points in the

---

[5] William Drabkin has argued that the Classical composers, cognisant of the special properties of the open string, deployed it so as to underscore special junctures in their string quartets. See his 'Beethoven and the Open String', *Music Analysis* 4 (1985), pp. 15-28; 'The Cello Part in Beethoven's Late Quartets', *Beethoven Forum* 7 (1999), pp. 45-66; 'Fingering in Haydn's Quartets', *Early Music* 16 (1988), pp. 50-57.
[6] William Drabkin, *A Reader's Guide to Haydn's Early String Quartets* (Westport, Connecticut: Greenwood Press, 2000), pp. 65-7.

fugal finales to op. 20 nos. 5 and 6, returns to the tonic are marked by full expositions; in the present quartet, Haydn confines the statements to *ritornelli* of one or two subjects. Obviously, punctuating the fugue with ancillary expositions would have compromised the drive towards its final resolution.

Let us turn now to the position of the finale within the whole quartet. Although the quartet is dominated by its finale, we will see that its teleological thrust (Model 2) is worked out within an elaborate series of rhymes and correspondences between the outer movements which perpetuates Model 1. The first movement, though a sonata form, presents its first-group material fugally, a tonic statement in the cello answered by the violin on the dominant. The proportions of the first movement (an exposition of forty-seven bars to a recapitulation of twenty-six, with a development of thirty-three) are grossly unbalanced for a sonata form, but are more appropriate to a Baroque work. In this way, the first movement anticipates, and is 'resolved' by, the proportions of the fugal finale, whose enormous middle section (a hundred and ten bars) dwarfs the exposition (eighteen bars) and coda (thirty-four bars). 'Resolution' here means cancelling the gap between form and content. Episodic form is now matched by contrapuntal content.

The motivic rhymes of op. 1 (Frame 1) are enriched here with a new tonal resonance. As in the rising and falling horn fanfares of 'The Hunt', the chromatic slide of the fugue subject (G-F sharp-F-E) inverts, and thereby resolves, the rising first subject of the opening movement (C-D-E-F sharp-G, bb. 6-7); a move from I to V is answered by a return from V to I, as if the two themes comprise the subject and answer of a gigantic fugal exposition. In the first movement, the chromatic slide is the source of the tonal obfuscation in its coda (bb. 98-102), as well as the central section of the *Menuetto* (bb. 21-28), in which the finale's semitone scale is first given its descending form. The finale reaches chromatic saturation at bb. 50-60, with sequential repetitions of the scale, detached from the subject. Much of the problem with the 'flatness' of the first movement, i.e. its quasi-Baroque continuity, is that the chromatic slide, E-F sharp-G and its dominant cognate B-C sharp-D, is distributed far too liberally. The exposition climbs to the dominant on at least four occasions: b. 7 in the tonic group, bb. 21 and 28 in the transition, b. 43 in the second group. As a result, the distinction between local and formal modulation – so crucial for a sonata exposition – is dissolved. This happens as a matter of course in the fugue, but leaves us with a nagging doubt as to whether the finale resolves these problems or actually compounds them. Does the finale effect a triumph of the Enlightenment over the Baroque, or, as Webster suggests, their 'coexistence'? [7]

Although much of the quartet's 'unfinished business' (Model 3) is unfolded within Frame 1 (pitch and motive), the originality of op. 20 is that Haydn starts to work with broader building-blocks of texture, harmonic genus, and topic (Frame 2). The quartet plays with oppositions between counterpoint and homophony, diatonic and chromatic, strict and free. The finale's coda (bb. 129-162) transforms the polyphonic texture into free figuration, and flattens out and inverts the G-F sharp-F-E motive into a 'white-note' rising scale (C-D-E) which evokes the very opening of the quartet (cello bb. 1-2). This juncture is important in Haydn's *oeuvre* because it exemplifies Haydn's increasing tendency to defer the 'moment of rhyme', as well as the point of resolution, from the head of the finale to its end. As we shall see, opp. 33 and 76 do this as well.

Op. 33 No. 5 in G

The op. 33 quartets of 1781 are composed in what Haydn himself termed 'a new and special way'. The accomplishment of the previous quartets notwithstanding, reception history has characterised this period as 'Haydn's first maturity' because of its striking synthesis of contrapuntal rigour, motivic logic, and the comic rhetoric of the rising 'popular style'.[8] The popular style allowed Haydn's finale to achieve two new things. First, its relaxed attitude to lyricism gave rise to a conception of resolution as dissolution of tension, so that a quartet could end with a dying fall. The finale of op. 33 no. 5 is a set of variations on a popular-style tune, and illustrates the function of repetitive forms (such as variations and rondos) to diffuse tension. [CD 20] The second novelty of this style is an enhanced sensitivity to formal convention (Frame 3). A broader understanding of periodic regu-

---

[7] See Webster, *op. cit.*, p. 300.
[8] Compare Denis McCaldin's and David Wyn Jones's discussions (pp. 43 ff. and 85) of the "new and special way" in which these quartets were composed (Ed.).

larity, together with greater differentiation between beginnings, middles and endings in Classical rhetoric, enabled structural dissonance to be resolved over a greater range. The theme of the *Allegretto* (a sixteen-bar song form, with two repeated eight-bar strains) contains a structural dissonance at the end of the first phrase, which rather than modulating conventionally to the dominant, ends with a half close on V of VI, a B major chord. [Ex. 6]

Ex. 6 op. 33 no. 5, IV, bb. 1-16

The modulation to D comes too late, two bars into the second phrase (b. 10). The deflection onto B is perpetuated by the three variations, and is only exorcised in the *presto* coda. The opposition between D major and E minor is actually encapsulated in bb. 1-2, where a turn figure on D (D-C sharp-D) is followed by one on E (E-D sharp-E). Again, the *Presto* not only removes these jarring accidentals, but grounds the turns on the tonic and, moreover, in the cello, as in the G-F sharp-G figures at b. 94.

The *locus classicus* of structural dissonance is the cadential opening. The first movement begins with a cadence, and this is put right at the close of the first phrase, b. 9, when the cadence is properly contextualised as an ending. [Ex. 7]

Ex. 7 op. 33 no. 5, I, bb. 1-9

This rising fourth figure (D-E-F sharp-G) returns in the finale, signalling both cyclical rhyme and closure. But the pacing of this return is what is notable. The figure is absent from the theme, is introduced in the second variation in the cello (b. 34), although not as a cadence, and is realised in the *Presto* (bb. 87-8) fully cadentially. [Ex. 8] The *ambitus* of the theme in bb. 1-16 of the finale had been cramped into the space of neighbour-note turn figures. When the thematic range is opened up into a rising fourth at b. 86, the effect is of a liberation. This point also marks the finale's 'moment of rhyme'. The cyclical return of the first-movement cadence is carefully graduated across the finale, so that the quartet winds up swallowing its tail. In more prosaic

Ex. 8 op. 33 no. 5, IV, bb. 33-35 and bb. 86-8

terms, although the movement is a set of variations – a repetitive form – it also unfolds a dynamic process.

Op. 54 No. 2 in C

The finale of this quartet is possibly Haydn's most radical experiment in form. It plays not only with ambiguities of structural function (Frame 3) but with the very identity of genre (Frame 4). Haydn had created hybrid movements before, as in the *Capriccio* of op. 20 no. 2, which mixes *ritornello* with sonata slow-movement form.[9] Placing a free form in the structurally sensitive position of the finale, however, represented an infinitely more radical step. [CD 21]

The finale splices together *Adagio* and *Presto* material in a way which invokes the character and role of at least five distinct genres: slow introduction; variation sets; slow movement; sonata-*allegro*; dance. Rather than being in a particular genre, the movement works through a series of generic connotations, and ends by transcending them all. The *Adagio* opening suggests an introduction (as in the finale of Mozart's G minor String Quin-

---

[9] Compare David Young's discussion of this movement on p. 58 (Ed.).

tet), but it ends at b. 8 with a tonic close (a proper introduction should end on a dominant). It is succeeded by more *Adagio*, signalling a possible variation form. But its treatment of the opening material is oblique; it is actually a thirty-two-bar song form. The expected repeat of the second strain (bb. 25-40) is interrupted by a C minor episode. The missing sixteen bars of *Adagio* are supplied, but with material extraneous to the song form (an intersplicing of a reprise of the *Adagio* introduction and the second half of the C minor episode, now in the tonic), and only after an even greater interruption: the *Presto*. The sudden irruption of a fast movement suggests that the assorted *Adagio* sections had constituted a slow introduction all along. But, once again, this interpretation is subverted by sixteen bars of *Adagio* which end the movement, and which retrospectively relegate the *Presto* to episodic status. Ironically, although the *Presto* introduces the most dramatic contrast into the movement, on closer inspection this contrast turns out to be illusory: the *Presto* is a literal variation on the *Adagio*. It is a thirty-two-bar song form – sixty-four bars with repeats – with interpolated retransitions (bb. 72-9; 97-103) and a coda (bb. 113-121). The correspondences between *Adagio* and *Presto* are exact:

Adagio:	9-16	17-24	25-32	33-40
Presto:	57-64	repeat	65-72	80-88

The *Presto* continues with further repetitions, which retrospectively point up the 'missing' sections of the *Adagio*, thus paving the way for the return of *Adagio* material at the end. The formal relationship between the *Adagio* and *Presto* is thus complementary: if the *Adagio* song-form is missing the conventional repeat of its second strain, then the *Presto* song-form is burdened with a superfluity of material – an extra twenty-four bars.

As if compensating for the elusive functional relationships between the *Adagio* and *Presto* sections, Haydn tantalises the listener with a plethora of motivic interconnections based on easily identifiable rising scale patterns. He renders these particularly audible with textural sign-posts; most strikingly, duets in thirds or sixths. The cello/viola duet which opens the finale (bb. 1-3) is complemented by the duet between the two violins which runs through most of the *Presto*. [Ex. 9]

Ex. 9 op. 54 no. 2, IV, bb. 1-6 and 57-64 [CD 21]

This process of complementation is not simply a matter of timbre but also of melodic *ambitus*: the original duet had been
intervallically constricted, only managing to climb as high as a
G, whereas the *Presto*'s scales are uninhibited, rising the full octave. This is why the *Presto* feels like the release of a coiled spring.

And yet, with a further twist of Haydn's paradox, these textural
and melodic correspondences operate between the *Presto* and
bb. 1-8 of the *Adagio, not* the thirty-two-bar song form which is
the *Presto*'s model. The motivic sign-posts are thereby self-de-
feating, since they cut across the harmonic and formal patterns
which bind the *Presto* to the *Adagio* song form.

How, then, does the listener make any sense of this finale?
By considering it in relation to the whole quartet. Problematic
as it is, in a curious way the finale is more stable than the first
movement on which its material is based. Bars 1-12 of the *Vivace*
foreshadow the antecedent-consequent period of bb. 1-8 of the
Adagio (the *Vivace* dotted minims become *Adagio* dotted semiquavers), but with irregular six-bar phrasing, and with the
destabilising entry of a third phrase on A flat at b. 13. Likewise,
the square circle-of-fifths episodes in the *Adagio* and *Presto* song-
forms (bb. 25-32 and 65-72) are the normative model for the
harmonically vagrant transition section of the *Vivace*, bb. 34-
54. The *Presto*'s duets echo the scales in thirds of the *Vivace*'s
second group, bb. 56-72. But while the *Presto* moves conventionally to the dominant, the *Vivace* duets simply circle the new
key in a way which fails to absorb the harmonic tensions of the
first group (the full reckoning is deferred till the coda of the
reprise). We now see that the relationship between first movement and finale is antithetical in an extraordinary way: the *Vivace*
is free on a local level, but strict formally (sonata form), whereas
the finale is perfectly conventional on the level of the phrase,
but *sui generis* as a form. Haydn's quartet offers a signal instance
of Model 4, whereby a finale transforms the entire ethos of a
first movement. The two movements are locked into such a state
of mutual dependency that it makes equal sense to say that the
first movement resolves the finale.

Op. 76 No. 3 in C ('The Emperor')

The six 'Erdödy' quartets op. 76 (1796-7) develop the symphonic style of writing Haydn had employed in the quartets
written during his visit to England (opp. 71 and 74) – chamber
music conceived for the public concert room. Haydn, the master of musical logic, adopts a more relaxed approach towards
sheer sonority as a vehicle for expression: double stopping, virtuoso figuration, and big rhetorical gestures. The string quartet
has travelled far from its origins as intellectual edification for

connoisseurs. This new communicative directness is expressed most dramatically on the level of 'narrative'. Three of these quartets (op. 76 no. 1 in G, no. 2 in D minor, and no. 3 in C) have a finale which begins in the minor and journeys towards an apotheosis in the major – the reflected light of *The Creation*. Although the narrative of light triumphing over darkness receives its paradigmatic formulation in Haydn's great oratorio, its presence can be felt in these instrumental works too. Nevertheless, there is an essential difference in the way this narrative is worked out: in *The Creation*, the turn from C minor to a resplendent C major occurs near the beginning of the work, whereas the quartets place this moment towards the end of their finale. Thus, in op. 76 nos. 2 and 3, the *minore* finale interrupts a work primarily in the major key. Haydn's narrative is not so much 'victory over adversity' (as in Beethoven's C minor Symphony), as the pastoral trope of 'idyll, storm, and restoration'.

The finale of op. 76 no. 3 is a fully-fledged sonata movement, the first we have looked at. [CD 22] Haydn's '*Creation* narrative' dictates that the 'turn to the light' happens twice: initially in the second group in the relative major (E flat), and then when this section is recapitulated in the tonic major (C). We will focus on how Haydn prepares this moment, and on how he extrapolates it from various key elements in the quartet, such as the celebrated 'Emperor's Hymn' ('Gott! Erhalte Franz den Kaiser'), which forms the basis for the set of variations in the slow movement and which gave the work its sobriquet.

The finale of the 'Emperor' begins with an arresting call to attention: three double-stopped hammer blows, *forte*, answered by a *piano* melody circling a rising third, C-E flat, first violin. [Ex. 10]

Ex. 10 op. 76 no. 3, IV, bb. 1-4

Not only do these four bars encapsulate the material of the entire movement; they also demarcate, with effortless efficiency, a conceptual opposition unfolded across its seventy-two-bar exposition. The first member of this oppositional pair, the hammer blows, signals opening, and appropriately dominates the tonic group. The second member of the opposition is the 'rising third', and it comes to the fore in the more lyrical second group. Since this is a monothematic exposition (compare with the first movement of op. 74 no. 1, also in C), this 'second group' is defined by the way it transforms first-group material, as well as by its new key area. We shall concentrate on this group, since its recapitulation will mark the quartet's ultimate resolution to the tonic major. It is unusually expansive (fifty-two bars to the first group's twenty), and divides into four broadly equal units of about twelve bars each.

The transitional first section, which we may call 'A' (bb. 21-32), is harmonically mobile, and unfolds the 'rising third' idea contrapuntally in all four parts. It settles into E flat major at b. 33 ('B'), segmenting the two-bar scale into a one-bar cadential idea deployed antiphonally. The stability of the new key is clinched at b. 46 ('C') with a resumption of the hammer-blow rhythmic figures, now sounding cadential rather than hortatory. These are covered by the first violin's triplet quaver figuration. The 'rising third' scale returns in the last section at b. 58 ('D'), although it is obscured by the continuation of the triplet quaver figuration. Crucial to the effect of this scale here is that its goal, the mediant G (viola, b. 60), glows against a solid tonic harmony. When this idea was introduced in C minor at bb. 3-8, the third of the scale had been consistently subverted by diminished chords.

An exhaustively forensic development section spills over into the recapitulation of the first group (bb. 119-151). In comparison, the reprise of the second group is relatively unchanged, although with three striking adjustments. First and foremost, it returns (from b. 152) in the key of C major. Second, its third section ('C'), originally characterised by the resumption of the hammer blows, is entirely omitted. This carries forward the drift from the hortatory to the lyric which we noted in the exposition. Third, the material in section 'D' (from b. 175) is redistributed, so that the 'rising third' scale is no longer covered by the triplet quaver figuration: it is lifted up to the top range of the viola and the first violin, and its apotheosis brings the quartet to a luminous close highlighting bright E naturals. Listen to the second-group reprise in its entirety.

Such is the popular appeal of the op. 76 quartets that one can easily overlook their highly experimental nature. In particular, they take forward the radical discovery of op. 54: the emancipation of form from content, and material from function. Let us go back to the tonic group of the exposition. Such declamatory gestures, swinging from I to V in the minor mode, sound like developmental retransitions. It is common for development sections in major-mode works to end in the tonic minor. Compare with the middle section of the minuet, bb. 21-32. This passage even shares the same material as these hammer blows: neighbour note figures around C (C-B-C) and G (G-A flat-G). The move into the 'Light' is achieved normatively in the *da capo* of the minuet, but in the quartet it happens initially (and prematurely) within the finale's second group in E flat, from b. 33. The E flat key chimes with the E flat parenthesis from the first movement's exposition, *strikingly also from b. 33*; indeed, the thematic material is also the same.

Listening 'bifocally' in this way, we have learned two things about the finale. On one level, despite surface appearances, it begins in *medias res*, and the exposition proper is deferred, paradoxically, to the relative major. This ambiguity is possible because of the movement's monothematicism – i.e. because the two groups share the same material. Second, we now know why the movement begins so unusually in the tonic minor. There is a further motivation for this key: it compensates for the lack of a normative *minore* variation in the slow movement. (For an example of a variation set which obeys this rule, see the *Andante grazioso* of op. 74 no. 2, which contains the obligatory central variation in B flat minor.) The connection between the finale and the 'Emperor's hymn' is in fact profound. We have seen that the coda, bb. 151 ff., presents the movement's resolution as a scale C-D-E, a climb towards the focal pitch E. This motif is of course the *incipit* of the hymn (G-A-B). The fourth variation in the second movement reharmonises the melody in E minor. Another reason, therefore, for the omission of the normative minor variation is that a G minor episode would have detracted from the projection of E natural.

In this finale, the five closural frames that we have explored throughout Haydn's quartets are all in evidence. The work is particularly notable for Haydn's renewed emphasis on miniature pitch cells (Frame 1), a procedure one would imagine to be alien to its formal breadth and extrovert rhetoric. The story of this quartet is very much an opposition between the pitches E flat and E natural, with their tonal correlatives of C minor (darkness) and C major (light). If Haydn could be said to have become a 'better' composer in the thirty years between op. 1 and op. 76, his achievement lay in harmonising his speculative bent as an abstract thinker with his obligations to his growing audience. The miracle of the finale to the 'Emperor' quartet is that an aesthetic narrative (Frame 5) is expressed via a motivic detail (Frame 1): a climb towards the light as a step from E flat to E.

JOSEPH HAYDN: INNOVATOR AND ARTIST

It is a truism of music historiography that innovation is not the same as artistic merit. Otherwise, we would accord figures such as Sammartini, Ordonez, Stamitz and J. C. Bach – the composers who invented the fundamentals of the Classical style – more honour than Mozart, Haydn or Beethoven. Bearing in mind this distinction, Haydn's finales should be given due credit for certain innovations which are generally attributed to Beethoven in his third period. Op. 1 no. 1: Haydn's integration of melodic ornamentation and harmonic structure anticipates the role of trills in many of Beethoven's finales, such as the *Arietta* of op. 111, and the *Grosse Fuge*. Op. 20 no. 2: the notion of the finale as centre of gravity lies behind Beethoven's *Hammerklavier* Sonata, as well as his C sharp minor quartet. Op. 33 no. 5: for a finale variation movement in which a cyclical return to the opening movement is progressively unfolded, see Beethoven's op. 109. Op. 54 no. 2: the most striking example of a hybrid *Adagio/Allegro* finale in Beethoven is actually an early work, 'La Malinconia' from his op. 18 no. 6 (but see also op. 110). Op. 76 no. 3: for a Beethoven finale which also begins with a retransition in the minor, see op. 127 (also in C minor).

By inventing these procedures, Haydn stretches the boundaries of the possible; he develops a language. Identifying these procedures, however, only serves to turn us back to the scores, to how they are used. Here, the guiding criterion for interpretation is not novelty but artistry. And here, Haydn and Beethoven (and Mozart too) are non-commensurable, because equally unique.

Performing Haydn's Quartets

Alan George

INTRODUCTION

It is an inescapable reality that (with the notable exception of *The Creation*) Haydn is not good 'box-office': certainly he cannot match the drawing-power of the three other Viennese 'Classics', and the replacing of a Haydn quartet with one by Mozart – particularly in the context of a less than popular programme – might well be reflected in increased ticket sales. Whether or not the audience (once actually there) would demonstrate a correspondingly heightened response to the music itself is a quite different matter, since many connoisseurs maintain that in general Mozart's quartets are less successful than his quintets, and less enjoyable to play or to listen to than those of Haydn. Is there an explanation for this phenomenon?

Music lovers are rightly fascinated by the actual human beings who created the sounds and feelings being communicated to them; and Haydn did lead a quieter, less colourful, less tragically abbreviated life than Mozart or Schubert (or even Beethoven). More to blame, perhaps, is an unfortunate attitude to Haydn – and to earlier repertoire in general – which pervades many performers, listeners, and promoters alike: include a symphony by Haydn in a concert which also contains one by Mahler, or one of his quartets followed by Smetana, Debussy, or even Brahms, and one has a playing field which is not exactly level. It is to be expected that Mahler's orchestra, for all its wonderful chamber-style subtleties, will trump Haydn's for sheer size and colour. The same cannot be said about the string quartet programmes, since the medium (or 'orchestration') is identical for every work. But is it? With the rise of the so-called 'chamber orchestra' a couple or more generations ago, and the subsequent evolution of 'Classical' orchestras using instruments and performing techniques of the period, such incongruous programme building has become less common, allowing both Haydn and Mahler to flourish to greater advantage in more sympathetic surroundings.

Would that the same enlightenment were generally in evidence in the quartet world. All too often professional string quartets are happy for 'their' sound to serve for whatever music they happen to be playing, perhaps even thinking it unnecessary to make any differentiation. But it should surely be self evident that applying the same richness of sound to Haydn as to, say, Tchaikovsky does no real service to the former, in the same way that his orchestral palette would be made to seem plain in direct comparison with the Russian master's. If we do not understand and acknowledge the vastly different resources available to composers of different eras, then it is inevitable that the earlier music can sound almost primitive in comparison. But change the scenario, elevate a late Haydn quartet to the prominence it would have received at the end of the eighteenth century, present it in a manner which befits its language, and suddenly there is the potential for these works to stand out as the pioneering, *innovative* masterpieces they must have seemed when they were new.

But how to accomplish this? Clearly the onus is mainly on the players themselves, and the motivation behind this essay is the desire to see Haydn's quartets achieve as much impact as their successors – *consistently* rather than merely sporadically. The first necessity is to remove Haydn from the now familiar spot at the start of a conventional three-quartet programme. At this point in a concert neither the performers nor the audience will be fully comfortable, or attuned to the ambience. If the players are accused of using Haydn to 'warm up', the audience is no less ready to concentrate on the music without distractions. So, invariably, it is Haydn who suffers. Sometimes (but increasingly less often) it is Mozart instead – but his unique appeal seems to be able to survive any maltreatment. In a nutshell, the cosy image of Haydn as the 'Father of the String Quartet' serves only to place him decisively at the *beginning* of the line, from which all else flourished.

There may be some truth here with regard to the Divertimenti from opp. 1 to 20. But let us not ignore the mutual and reciprocal influence which bounced back and forth from Haydn to Mozart following the former's op. 33; and the reality that Mozart was actually dead by the time Haydn came to write his op. 71 would suggest that his last fourteen and a half quartets must in many ways have advanced beyond anything Mozart contributed to the medium – and not a little beyond Beethoven's earliest efforts as well. A programme of eighteenth-century string quartets could quite justifiably *conclude* with a work from Haydn's op. 76 or op. 77 – even if Mozart or a Beethoven op. 18 were also on the programme. In such a context we suddenly become more aware of the true stature of his last quartets, the wisdom, the imagination, the vision.

Additionally, if we happen to be using the type of instruments those composers were familiar with, we might realise not only how wonderfully Haydn exploited their potential, but recognise the demands he made on them as well – which has long been the prerogative of Beethoven alone. In his op. 71 set Haydn was, probably for the first time, writing with the public concert room in mind, and his attempts to bring the sonority of the orchestra into the string quartet would undoubtedly have placed a strain on players and instruments alike; with the advantage of our powerful metal strings and modern bows, that is not easy to envisage today. Pieces such as Beethoven's *Grosse Fuge*, or much of the F minor quartet op. 95 are – like most other Beethoven – a struggle to play on any instrument. This is not the case with Haydn's op. 71. When, however, these works are played on a Baroque violin (which may well have been all that was yet available to someone like Salomon in far off London), Haydn is suddenly revealed as a revolutionary.

Having begun by examining our fundamental approach to Haydn's quartets, we are prepared to programme them more sensitively, and to attempt to play them in a more considerate manner. While the former is not really so difficult, we should now look at how we might embark on the latter.

THE TEXT

The obvious starting point is the text. Most of us were brought up on the Peters' *30 berühmte Quartette*, two volumes of the most 'celebrated' Haydn quartets in those unmistakable green covers. Indeed, the most enterprising of us went on to volumes III and IV (*sämtliche Quartette*) to complete our libraries (with a bit of detective work to find one's way round their idiosyncratic numbering system). Nowadays, editors are expected to reveal precisely what they have contributed to the text. The Peters' team, however, (probably with the best will in the world) set about producing an edition which may well have facilitated the execution of the notes, but succeeded ultimately in obscuring what Haydn actually wrote down. (I deliberately refer to a 'team' because, although only two editors are named, the impression is sometimes of four members of a less than communicative quartet who have worked on their own parts in isolation and have put in their own suggestions: co-ordination of editorial bowings, dynamics, articulation, etc. is not always evident.) Indeed, there was a certain vagueness as to the sources for this edition, but with the help of the slightly cleaner Eulenberg miniature scores one could at least remove some of the accumulated tarnish – the *sämtliche* volumes seemed less heavily edited than the others, perhaps because these works were considered to be of less interest to amateurs.

Since 1968, two far more scholarly editions have gradually appeared, and it is these which must now at all times supersede the old Peters. They are published respectively by Doblinger and Henle, both highly respected compilers of Urtext editions. Both identify their sources, which are generally common to each, and critical reports are also available, as are scores of every work. In the case of Henle, these form part of their *Complete Edition of Joseph Haydn's Works*, and for some time their sets of parts held a practical advantage over Doblinger through being printed in volumes by opus number. With the latter one was faced with the considerable expense of having to buy each quartet individually, which meant that it was more economical to obtain the miniature score, and laboriously to correct one's Peters part from it. Doblinger have now adopted the same system, and since their editors are two of our most distinguished Haydn authorities, H. C. Robbins Landon and Reginald Barrett-Ayres, this publisher could claim to have the edge. In any case, it is so much easier to read from clean Urtext material than the cluttered Peters edition, even if page turns can at times be less than considerately placed.

If one wants to play the *Seven Last Words*, however, Peters (volume IV) is still the only choice; it is reasonably clean, and one can check details with the Eulenberg score, or a score of the oratorio version. Robbins Landon tells me there is no Urtext edition of the quartet version, and the only other source is the first edition, published by Artaria, which is preserved in the British Library, as well as in the Gesellschaft der Musikfreunde in Vienna.

INSTRUMENTS AND BOWS

It is by no means essential that historical instruments be employed in order to do justice to Haydn's music, even if specialists or purists might try to persuade one otherwise (the present writer was for many years a 'purist', if not a 'specialist'). But there is no doubt that the more appropriate the equipment, the nearer one can get to the sounds that years of painstaking scholarship suggest Haydn might have recognised. Instruments with smaller bass bar, sound post, bridge and tailpiece, flatter neck, gut strings (plain or wound), together with a lighter, 'transitional' bow – or even a convex 'Baroque' bow – have the *potential* to produce colours all of their own. There must be an emphasis on 'potential', because the *techniques* for realising these sounds are yet more obligatory (see the following section). One could make a strong case for the actual sound of the music being no less important than the pitches, rhythms, and dynamics, all of which can be written down with a degree of accuracy. Our Western system of notation, however, is not able to indicate precise sounds and colours, beyond naming the required instrument(s) at the head of the score; these have changed so substantially since Haydn's day (in some cases out of all recognition, like the piano) that we might well feel a compulsion to seek out a specific musical truth and try to get as close to those sounds as we possibly can.

Regrettably, very few professional string quartets have taken it upon themselves to assume a mantle of leadership with regard to the use of period instruments; nevertheless, there are those with the conscience at least to take account of some of the stylistic information uncovered by other, more enquiring musicians. It has to be admitted that the old instruments do bring a number of extra hazards. Intonation is perhaps the most likely danger, because of the greater tendency of gut strings to go out of tune, together with the heightened examination of left-hand accuracy afforded by a more sparing use of vibrato. Gut is especially sensitive to changes of temperature and humidity, so that damp, hot or cold conditions can make gut strings reluctant to speak readily, with resultant embarrassing squeaks!

There is also the fear that listeners – especially those of less enterprising outlook – will not take kindly to the loss of their much-loved sumptuousness of sound; and there are enough quartet players who are themselves not prepared to relinquish this indulgent type of noise in earlier music. One's concept of what is, or is not, beautiful can be modified with surprising ease, if one is willing to listen without prejudice. There is nothing to compare with the resonance and purity produced by four gut-strung instruments sounding a chord perfectly in tune together. Haydn's understanding of how string instruments work with each other, particularly through his resourceful spacing of the parts, affords us this aural pleasure rather more often than with other composers; so there is every reason for his quartets to be the trigger for taking the plunge. But unfortunately, for the time being, the risks seem to present too great a barrier, despite the fact that the rewards can make them well worth the taking. Even if resistance still prevails, however, it is well worth adopting a set of Classical instruments for private study.

In the Fitzwilliam Quartet, although we have performed extensively on contemporary instruments, from Purcell to Brahms, we would be the first to acknowledge that appropriate instruments and appropriate conditions are not always going to coincide. We do occasionally change instruments during the interval of a widely mixed programme, but this can sometimes be foolhardy. Cold, damp churches in January, or vast, acoustically dead multi-purpose halls in large American cities have, of late, persuaded us to compromise, but only with regard to the instruments themselves. We find that, having studied and performed all our earlier repertoire on gut, we are able to retain enough of the sounds in our heads to go some way towards reproducing them on the more modern set-up when required.

This is not to suggest that modern instruments can be made to sound exactly like old ones, even though some players claim that their 'normal' instruments provide a broad enough palette to make a change superfluous. However wide the range of sounds, it can never quite match those available from gut strings and once again, I cannot emphasise strongly enough the importance of previous experience of how gut *feels* and resonates. One of the advantages of the 'real thing' is that one need not be inhibited by fear of playing too loudly, or of overstepping the boundaries of 'Classical taste'. Because we know that only so much volume was available to Haydn, the tendency has been to play his music in a scaled-down manner, with a resultant loss of energy, vibrancy, and character. I recently heard a fine performance of a late Haydn quartet by one of our younger established groups, noted for the power of their playing. They had evidently taken great care to incorporate an awareness of eighteenth-century style, and the result was pleasingly idiomatic and clean, but it lacked panache and real imagination. With the early instruments one can really 'lay in' without fear; the gut itself will let you know when you have overstepped the mark.

TECHNIQUES, ARTICULATION, NOTATION

One praiseworthy virtue of the performance to which I refer above was the quartet's toning down of their normally generous vibrato. Herein lies a prerequisite for playing any eighteenth-century music, yet it is extraordinary how many string quartets are unable – or unwilling – to adapt to the requirements of that epoch. A vibrato-orientated sound is unpleasant enough at any time. As recently as 1921 Leopold Auer writes that "[vibrato] is an effect, an embellishment; it can lend a touch of divine pathos, but only if the player has cultivated a delicate sense of proportion in the use of it."[1] In eighteenth-century repertoire such excess is quite unacceptable. In his *Versuch einer gründlichen Violinschule* (1756), Leopold Mozart entreats us:

> the tremolo [i.e. vibrato] must only be used at places where nature herself would produce it... it would be an error if every note were played with the tremolo. Performers there are who tremble consistently on each note as if they had the palsy.[2]

Disease is evidently rife among the quartet playing fraternity! But it is not so much the *consistency* of vibrato which is so at odds with the musical language (Leopold's observation implies that some players *did* vibrate continuously) but the *magnitude*, where purity of pitch and sound is compromised, where clarity of line is lost in a dense homogeneity, and where everything is supplemented by persistent modern-style *legato*.

This latter – another common evil – is utterly at odds with Leopold's oft-repeated instructions to play slurred notes with a stress on the first, the rest then following "even more and more quietly". The natural contours of a bow stroke are destroyed in a misguided quest for evenness of tone, and while such playing may well be at one with music of more recent times, it has no place in

---

[1] Leopold Auer, *Violin Playing As I Teach It* (New York: Frederick A. Stokes, 1921).
[2] Leopold Mozart, *Versuch einer gründlichen Violinschule* (Augsburg, 1756), translated by Editha Knocker as *A Treatise on the Fundamental Principles of Playing the Violin*, 2nd edition (London: Oxford University Press, 1967).

eighteenth-century expression. To apply today's conventions to music of former centuries is the equivalent of the much-maligned Englishman holidaying abroad, speaking French with an English accent. Just as the letters of the alphabet imply different sounds in different languages, so do symbols on a page of music convey different instructions in different eras. It is vital to grasp the principle that solid, seamless, sustained tone is the antithesis of the lighter, airier, more contoured phrasing and articulation favoured little more than a hundred years ago. To modern ears, this can appear to suggest a lack of line, a chopped-up approach to phrasing, and it is certainly true that some early music practitioners can be over-zealous in their adherence to the rule book. But when executed correctly and tastefully this approach should be persuasive enough to any listener prepared to condone the reversing of long-held but misplaced traditions.

The principle needs also to be extended to the general use of the bow, and in particular to the embracing of a lighter manner of articulation – Leopold implores us "not to play continuously with a lagging, heavy stroke". These more *detaché* types of bow stroke are less fashionable now, and less easily mastered. But, once again, the simplest way to understand the concept is to try an earlier bow, to let its weight and balance work naturally, to feel and listen to what it does and to learn from it. Our modern bows, with their heavier heads, are much more adept at sustaining right to the tip than their older counterparts. One must remember that phrasing and articulation arose very much from the equipment the players were familiar with, so that when Beethoven confronted the *status quo* head-on, makers were required to build instruments and bows which could meet the new demands, and players in turn were forced to extend their technical capabilities in order to face this challenge. What has emerged are bows and bowing skills which enable a down-bow and an up-bow to sound the same, making them interchangeable and thus negating the most basic and ancient rule of all, whereby a strong beat (*nota buona*) should be taken with a down-bow, and up-beats with up-bows. Music from this period sounds all the more natural and fluid if one does not lose sight of this simple directive; the hierarchy of beats within a bar, and bars within a phrase, should rarely be overturned, and bowing should be selected judiciously in order to preserve these principles.

Mention has already been made of how the slur sign, as used

by Haydn and his contemporaries, conveyed a more complex meaning than its use over the past century – we now simply 'slur' two or more notes together within the same bow stroke. Similarly, other details of notation must be grasped if players are not to give an inaccurate rendition of the composer's intentions. To look further at the use of this slur sign, for example, we must understand that, when two or more notes of the same pitch are grouped under one slur, the intention is not necessarily the same as with what we now call a 'tie'. This sign often – although not always (discretion plays a part as well) – means that each note is articulated with a slight release and reapplication of pressure during the *travelling* bow stroke (this effect is particularly significant – and problematical – with Beethoven in, for example, the main subject of the *Grosse Fuge*). Similarly, notes grouped under a slur but apparently separated by dots imply the same bow stroke, giving a sound that is continuous but that 'dips' (rather than notes that are separated by silence) as in the very opening of the 'Bird' Quartet, op. 33 no. 3.

Discretion – and experience – also come into play when we attempt to interpret Haydn's often sparing use of slurs. Does he expect notes to be slurred only when indicated, or does he assume the performers know from the context when they should be added? In Chapter Four of his *Versuch*, Leopold Mozart gives examples of when slurs should be applied: to notes at close intervals, and to reverse-dotted rhythms, to name but two – "depending on the cantilena of the piece and on the good taste and sound judgment of the performer". It is clear that musicians in Haydn's day were so well schooled in every facet of their art that such choices would be a normal part of their craft. One should remember that they were required to play only compositions of their own time, unlike the modern exponent who is faced by an almost bewildering range of idioms; so perhaps, after all, one should not be too critical of those who settle for an all-purpose method of playing.

Further decisions have to be made with regard to dynamics, because Haydn is no more generous with these than with slurs. Certainly in the Baroque era it was rarely necessary for composers to add dynamic markings, simply because the players would know instinctively what was expected. When Bach, for example, does notate a dynamic it is often where there might be a degree of doubt. Haydn seems to have continued this tradition, at the same time handing his players the opportunity to contribute to the creative process by bringing their powers of imagination into play.

As to the vexed question of repeats, could this be yet another instance where eighteenth-century convention allows the players to make choices? Or are repeat signs, like the notes themselves, instructions to be obeyed diligently? In the past there has been a very lax attitude to repeats, but the last couple of decades have witnessed a notably less cavalier approach, so much so that for a time the BBC insisted that any performance of a Haydn quartet should include every notated repeat. This policy has since moved a stage further with the theory that repeats should also be taken during the *da capo* of a minuet/scherzo. Since instances began to appear where a *da capo* was specifically instructed to be made *without* repeats (Beethoven was at pains to ensure that this instruction was obeyed in the Scherzo of his Ninth Symphony), the implication seems to be that repeats were expected unless otherwise indicated. One can also cite instances in Haydn's minuets (e.g. op. 77 no. 1, or the 'London' Symphony) where the composer decides to *vary* a repeat, which necessitated his writing the section out again – meaning, of course, that on the *da capo*, the relevant section will again be heard twice. Might this indicate something about the correct shape of these movements: AABB-CCDD-*AABB* rather than AABB-CCDD-*AB*?

With regard to the traditional design of movements other than the minuet and trio/scherzo and trio, it is self-evident that what we now call 'sonata form' originated in a binary structure whose two sections were played twice. Because the two 'halves' had, by the end of the eighteenth century, become far less equal in length, plenty of examples arise where composers have themselves made the choice as to when a section should not be repeated – a practice which became more and more common over the ensuing hundred or so years. Even Shostakovich occasionally decided to call for an exposition repeat while, conversely, Mozart, in revising his 'Haffner' Symphony, removed both repeats in the first movement. With the op. 64 quartets it is still the norm for Haydn to mark both halves of the outer movements with repeats but thereafter he becomes more discriminating, starting with the finales. The first three quartets of op. 76 still call for the second half of the first movement to be repeated – in nos. 2 and 3 with first-time bars as well, emphasising that this is no mindless relic of convention – but by op. 77 both outer movements are decidedly AAB. (It is, however, interesting to note that the traditional AABB form survived at least as far as Beethoven's 'Rasumovsky' quartets where, after a first movement with no repeats in no. 1, he calls for two in the corresponding place in no. 2, together with enormous first-time bars for both; if these repeats are not observed, one leaves out a significant chunk of Beethoven's music at one's peril.) The point to emphasise is that, by crediting great composers with being more precise about repeats than we often care to admit, we might thereby learn that eighteenth-century quartets are often on as large a scale as their successors. The only qualification is that, until Haydn's op. 71, quartets were principally designed to be played in private rather than performed in public (the earlier divertimenti might even have served as background entertainment). Moreover, we cannot deny that we now live at a more hectic pace than our forefathers, so consideration for a correspondingly shorter span of concentration among listeners could at times justify judicious selection of repeats.

There is no doubt that Haydn thought *through* the medium when composing his quartets, which is one of many reasons why they are so satisfying to play. He was, of course, no mean violinist himself – and a quartet player, too, having famously collaborated with Dittersdorf, Mozart on viola, and the Bohemian cellist Vanhal in the birth of the six quartets dedicated to him by none other than the group's viola player! Evidence, if it be needed, of his practical approach to this *genre* can be found in the various fingerings he contributed, usually to the first violin part. Not only do these provide precious insight as to how he played himself, but there are instances of how the fingering he stipulates forms an integral part of the notation. Examples of this can be found in the Trio of op. 64 no. 6, or in the first movement of op. 74 no. 3; in both cases it is evident from the fingering – on one string – that a *portamento*, or even a *glissando*, is inevitable, which of course has serious implications as to how and when these effects might otherwise be employed.[3]

ORNAMENTATION, EMBELLISHMENT, CADENZAS

These fall into two categories: those that are notated, and

---

[3] See William Drabkin, 'Fingering in Haydn's Quartets', *Early Music* 16 (1988), pp. 50-57.

those which are improvised and added by the performer. Leopold
Mozart does not separate the two as conveniently as we might
have hoped, except that his instructions and examples as to how
and when they should be employed are extensive and painstaking. While Chapter XI of *Versuch* deals with a full array of em-
bellishments, of which only the various types of mordent (and
of course the *tremolo*) are especially relevant to Haydn, the whole
of Chapter IX is devoted to the *appoggiatura*, and Chapter X to
the trill – how they should be executed, and when they should
be applied (in addition to those places where they are actually
notated). I thoroughly recommend these invaluable essays, which
are too detailed to be meaningfully summarised here. I am, however, able to pass on a few very basic principles:

> 1. Trills always begin on the upper note [it is only towards the
> end of the century that exceptions begin to suggest themselves].

> 2. Mordents are unaccented: 'the stress of the tone falls on the
> note itself, while the mordent, on the contrary, is slurred quite
> softly and very quickly *on* to the principal note'.

> 3. Do not be tempted to embellish indiscriminately: 'All these
> decorations are used... only when playing a solo, at the right
> time, and only for variety in often-repeated and similar passages.'

During the pioneering years of the Early Music movement,
it became the norm to contrive to play all *appoggiature* and
mordents on the beat with a stress, as if a century of wrongly
interpreted 'grace notes' needed to be corrected. But Leopold
Mozart crucially divides the former into 'long' and 'short' vari-
eties: the latter

> is made as rapidly as possible and is not attacked strongly... the
> stress falls not on the *appoggiatura* but on the principal note. [But
> which is which? He goes on to say that] it is as clear as daylight
> that a violinist must know well how to decide whether the com-
> poser has intended any ornamentation, and if so, what kind!.

'Daylight' can only realistically be gained through a study of
Leopold Mozart's treatise, an understanding of both the melodic and harmonic principles involved, and the subsequent practical application of those principles to relevant passages of music. Thereafter experience, imagination, and sheer force of habit
can be increasingly relied upon.
The same could be said with regard to whether, and at what

point, a short cadenza might be desirable. One or more *fermata* signs can prove tempting – in the Minuet of op. 77 no. 2, for example, or near the end of op. 71 no. 2. But even then a degree of restraint is desirable; brevity is always mandatory, and silence is frequently more effective than display.

TEMPO

   A discussion of tempo brings us to one of the more contentious aspects of performance practice – controversial in any era, in fact, but increasingly so the further one moves into the past. Johann Nepomuk Mälzel's invention of the metronome in 1816 enabled composers to add precision to this hitherto vague aspect of musical notation – and with what alacrity and enthusiasm Beethoven grasped this opportunity. Yet the majority of performers are still sceptical of, if not downright opposed to, the 'tyranny' of the metronome, despite Beethoven's frequent plaudits in his letters. Whether or not we choose to respect his notated tempi, we should at least accept that they give us a good idea of the speed at which music was generally played at that time (and indeed earlier), as do surviving accounts by such artists as Czerny and Hummel. And whilst it would be easy to deduce that musicians of the Classical era tended to play their own music faster than we do today, there are plenty of examples to refute such a generalisation; the finales of Beethoven's fifth, sixth and seventh symphonies, or the slow sections of op. 18 no. 6 are marked to be played at a much slower tempo than might have been expected. Beethoven's dramatically confrontational spirit undoubtedly exerted a powerful influence on tempo as well, if we are to accept Leopold Mozart's explanation of *Allegro* as indicating 'a cheerful though not too hurried a tempo'. While this description hardly applies to Beethoven's *Allegros*, especially those unequivocally qualified by a metronome mark, it would seem to fit Haydn's perfectly; indeed, many modern-day performances do not allow Haydn's quicker movements enough breathing space. But it seems certain that our concept of the minuet has drifted very wide of the mark, if Czerny's suggested metronome marks for his piano arrangements of Haydn's 'London' symphonies are to be respected. Furthermore, one of Haydn's own tiny pieces for mechanical clock happens to consist of the same melody as the minuet of op. 54 no. 2: assuming the machinery is functioning correctly, we have the piece played at exactly the tempo that the composer intended. It is true that in his first two sets of quartets (the Divertimenti opp. 1 and 2) there are invariably two minuets of a contrasting type; but it was the quicker, rather than the slower, of these which eventually gained precedence. And if we follow Czerny's recommendations we find that it was Haydn, rather than Beethoven, who truly invented the scherzo, for there is far less distance to travel between the *Presto* minuets in Haydn's op. 77 and the Scherzo of Beethoven's op. 18 no. 1 than was once supposed.

The greatest discrepancy which has evolved over the years concerns slower movements. This is particularly the case with those marked *Andante*, which as we all know (even without Leopold Mozart's help) indicates a natural walking pace. In other words, the eighteenth-century *Andante* is not really a slow movement at all, and one has to question how many performances of such movements today one could comfortably 'stroll along' to. A similar – and completely inappropriate – gravity is also too often applied to Haydn's *Adagio* movements which, for the most part, contain his most profoundly lyrical outpourings. Could one really 'sing along' with so many of the doleful renditions on offer? A certain confusion with regard to slow tempi might arise through Haydn's choice of notation. If, for example, one compares the *Adagio* of the G major quartet, op. 77 no. 1 with the *Andante* in its F major companion, op. 77 no. 2, one finds that the actual crotchet pulse in the former would have to be sounded at an almost unsustainably slow tempo for it to relate to supposedly faster crotchets in the latter. From this, it should be self evident that Haydn tends not to think in the same note denominations for *Andante* and *Adagio* movements.

The lurking pitfall is to equate slowness with profundity, and nowhere will the performer be ensnared more readily than in Haydn's *The Seven Last Words from the Cross*, op. 51, the remarkable series of slow meditations on Christ's final utterances at Calvary. The composer himself wrote:

> The task of producing a succession of seven *Adagios*, each of which was to last about ten minutes, without wearying the listener, was no easy one; and I soon found that I could not keep to the prescribed duration...[4]

[4] Preface to version for soloists, chorus and orchestra, Breitkopf & Härtel, 1801.

which presumably means that the movements ended up shorter than planned. Whatever, then, would Haydn have made of most present-day interpretations of *Adagio, Lento* and *Largo*? The discrepancy in approach is underlined by two recent recordings which manage to disagree by as much as ten minutes over the complete work (more than the duration of an entire movement).

The variety Haydn achieves within *The Seven Last Words*, despite the constraints of his task, has to be heard to be believed, and yet it is realised all too rarely. The same can be said of his slow movements right across the board. The sheer depth of human expression enclosed within the slow movements of, for example, the two op. 77 quartets is in no way enhanced by drawing them out in the manner of a timeless Bruckner *Adagio*. Rather they should speak simply and humbly at a naturally flowing pace, free of strain and misplaced tension.

SPIRIT AND EXPRESSION

Listen to the sublime *Andante* of op. 77 no. 2 and ask whether there can be a more heartwarming expression of the deepest human spirit; listen to its crazy off-beat Menuet (in effect a scherzo) or its rustic, earthy finale, and ask whether energy, wit, and sheer exuberance could ever be given a more poignant voice. Since all this follows an opening *Allegro* of intellectual mastery and complexity, of grandeur and passion, presented in a language so utterly fresh and communicative, one can only conclude that here is a work that is so all-embracing that it truly has everything.

Is this why for some (including the present writer), Haydn's op. 77 no. 2 remains one of the greatest string quartets ever written? The answer must be, not entirely, since this work is also one of the most fulfilling in the whole repertoire for the quartet player. The purpose of this chapter has been to focus on aspects of *performing* Haydn's quartets, and it is particularly through the performer (as well as the listener and the scholar) that this vast body of music should be viewed. The string quartet originated, after all, in the 'chamber' for the domestic pursuit of pleasure through playing music in the company of friends. The ensemble of which I have been a member for over thirty years [the Fitzwilliam Quartet] is still able to work with such ideals in mind, and it is through these ideals that we judge Haydn's quartets to be more satisfying than most others.

The qualities so evident in our beloved F major were not, of course, achieved overnight. When we go back to op. 1, as we are frequently glad to do, we are not only aware of the huge extent to which Haydn evolved as a composer over a period of forty years, but also of how, at the age of sixty-seven, wiser and more worldly, he still relates to us as very much the same human being. In the C major quartet op. 1 no. 6, for example, one will find no less energy and wit in the outer movements, no shortage of grace and spirit in the minuets, no less exquisite charm and poignancy in the violin solo of the serenade-like *Adagio* than in its later, more sophisticated, counterpart. Therefore in playing these early divertimenti (which were conceived for the players' gratification, rather than for attentive and dutiful listening), we should do well not to treat them with reduced esteem, but instead be willing to adapt our playing to a substantially earlier, perhaps more archaic, but no less committed, style of execution.

By working through the full body of Haydn's quartets, one is able to experience his creative language developing, expanding, and deepening. If one is sensitive to this process, it can also inform and enrich one's playing in precisely the same manner, so that one gradually acquires an appropriate mode of execution for each set of quartets. How could the emancipated textures at the opening of op. 20 no. 2, for example, fail to inspire a new feeling for sonority within the ensemble? How could one not search for new hues and shades with each amazing modulation in the *Fantasia* of op. 76 no. 6?

Haydn's reputation has for too long suffered beyond the horizons he himself broadened; his achievements have too often been eclipsed by those of his successors. It was only natural that, as one of the great innovators, he should create not only a magnificent treasury of music himself but also limitless possibilities on which others might build. If Mozart was big enough to acknowledge Haydn's massive influence, then we should all strive to follow his example. While he may never quite equal the popular appeal of his younger friend, the HaydnFest in Manchester in January 1999 went a long way towards reminding us of his towering presence in our musical history and heritage. The music speaks for itself, but the performers' mission must be the responsibility of projecting it in the best possible light.

Chronological List of Haydn's String Quartets

Op./No.	Hoboken No.[1]	Key	Date Composed	Remarks
1			c1757-59?	
1/1	III:1	B flat		'La chasse'
1/2	III:2	E flat		
1/3	III:3	D		
1/4	III:4	G		
1/0	II:6	E flat		
1/6	III:6	C		
2			c1760-62?	
2/1	III:7	A		
2/2	III:8	E		
2/4	III:10	F		
2/6	III:12	B flat		
9			1769-70?	
9/1	III:19	C		
9/2	III:20	E flat		
9/3	III:21	G		
9/4	III:22	D minor		
9/5	III:23	B flat		
9/6	III:24	A		
17			1771	
17/1	III:25	E		
17/2	III:26	F		
17/3	III:27	E flat		
17/4	III:28	C minor		
17/5	III:29	G		'Recitative'
17/6	III:30	D		

[1] Anthony van Hoboken, *Joseph Haydn: Thematisch-bibliographisches Werkverzeichnis*, vol. 1 (Mainz: B. Schott's Söhne, 1957).

20			1772	'Sun' Quartets *from an illustration of the sun on the Hummel print of 1779*
20/1	III:31	E flat		
20/2	III:32	C		
20/3	III:33	G minor		
20/4	III:34	D		
20/5	III:35	F minor		
20/6	III:36	A		
33			1781	'Russian' Quartets *from the dedication to Grand Duke Paul Petrovich of Russia*
33/1	III:37	B minor		
33/2	III:38	E flat		'The Joke'
33/3	III:39	C		'The Bird'
33/4	III:40	B flat		
33/5	III:41	G		'How Do You Do?'
33/6	III:42	D		
42	III:43	D minor	1785	
50			1787	'Prussian Quartets' *from the dedication to King Frederick William II of Prussia*
50/1	III:44	B flat		
50/2	III:45	C		
50/3	III:46	E flat		
50/4	III:47	F sharp minor		
50/5	III:48	F		II: 'A Dream'
50/6	III:49	D		'The Frog'

54			1788	'Tost' Quartets i *from the dedication to the violinist Johann Tost*
54/1	III:58	G		
54/2	III:57	C		
54/3	III:59	E		
55			1788	'Tost' Quartets ii
55/1	III:60	A		
55/2	III61	F minor		'The Razor'
55/3	III:62	B flat		
64			1790	'Tost' Quartets iii
64/1	III:65	C		
64/2	III:68	B minor		
64/3	III67	B flat		
64/4	III:66	G		
64/5	III:63	D		'The Lark'
64/6	III:64	E flat		
71			1793	'Apponyi' Quartets i *from the dedication to Count Anton Georg Apponyi*
71/1	III:69	B flat		
71/2	III:70	D		
71/3	III:71	E flat		
74			1793	'Apponyi' Quartets ii
74/1	III:72	C		
74/2	III:73	F		
74/3	III:74	G minor		'The Rider'
76			1797	'Erdödy' Quartets *from the dedication to Count Joseph Erdödy*
76/1	III:75	G		
76/2	III:76	D minor		'Fifths'

76/3	III:77	C		'Emperor' *from II, which uses 'Gott erhalte Franz den Kaiser' as its theme*
76/4	III:78	B flat		'Sunrise' *from opening theme*
76/5	III:79	D		
76/6	III:80	E flat		
77			1799	'Lobkowitz' Quartets *from the dedication to Price Franz Joseph Maximilian Lobkowitz*
77/1	III:81	G		
77/2	III:82	F		
103	III:83	D minor	1803	Unfinished: *Movements II & III only (B flat and D minor)*

List of Printed Musical Examples

Extracts from the following string quartets by Joseph Haydn appear in Chapters II-V of this volume.

OP. 1 NO. 1 IN B FLAT ('LA CHASSE')
Movement	I	bb. 1-24	pp. 37-8
		bb. 25-28	p. 105
	IV	bb. 1-26	pp. 82-3
		bb. 27-42	pp. 84-5
	V	bb. 1-17	pp. 102-3
		bb. 28-44	p. 104

© Copyright 1979 by Ludwig Doblinger (Bernard Herzmansky) K.G., Wien-München. Reproduced by permission of Alfred A. Kalmus Ltd., London.

OP. 1 NO. 6 IN C
Movement	III	bb. 1-26	pp. 64-5

© Copyright 1979 by Ludwig Doblinger (Bernard Herzmansky) K.G., Wien-München. Reproduced by permission of Alfred A. Kalmus Ltd., London.

OP. 17 NO. 4 IN C MINOR
Movement	I	bb. 1-2	p. 39
		bb. 9-10 & 20-21	p. 40
		bb. 53-4, 62-3 & 76-86	p. 41
		bb. 120-3	p. 42

© Copyright 1988 by Ludwig Doblinger (Bernard Herzmansky) K.G., Wien-München. Reproduced by permission of Alfred A. Kalmus Ltd., London.

OP. 20 NO. 2 IN C
Movement	II	bb. 1-4	p. 66
		bb. 5-8	pp. 66-7
		bb. 34-37	pp. 67-8
	IV	bb. 1-15	pp. 106-7
		bb. 150-62	pp. 108

© Copyright 1981 by Ludwig Doblinger (Bernard Herzmansky) K.G., Wien-München. Reproduced by permission of Alfred A. Kalmus Ltd., London.

OP. 20 NO. 4 IN D
Movement II   bb. 1-18   p. 70

OP. 33 NO. 2 IN E FLAT ('THE JOKE')
Movement I   bb. 1-8   pp. 44-5
         II   bb. 1-34   pp. 86-7
                   bb. 35-68*   pp. 90-1

(* These same bars from the Edition Peters score are reproduced on p. 89)

OP. 33 NO. 5 IN G ('HOW DO YOU DO?')
Movement I   bb. 1-9   p. 112
         IV   bb. 1-16   p. 111
                   bb. 33-5 & 86-8   p.113

OP. 54 NO. 2 IN C
Movement II   bb. 1-18   pp. 71-2
         IV   bb. 1-6 & 57-64   p. 115

OP. 55 NO. 2 IN F MINOR ('THE RAZOR')
Movement I   bb. 1-8   p. 77
                   bb. 27-35   p. 78

OP. 64 NO. 5 IN D ('THE LARK')
Movement I   bb. 1-12   p. 48
                   bb. 35-42   pp. 48-9
                   bb. 50-9   p. 49
                   bb. 60-4   p. 50

II   bb. 1-41   pp. 72-4
          bb. 51-8   pp. 74-5

OP. 74 NO. 3 IN G MINOR ('THE RIDER')
Movement II   bb. 1-37   pp. 75-6

OP. 76 NO. 3 IN C ('THE EMPEROR')
Movement IV   bb. 1-4   p. 117

OP. 76 NO. 4 IN B FLAT ('THE SUNRISE')
Movement I   bb. 1-15   p. 53-4
                  bb. 37-40   p. 55
                  bb. 66-7   p. 52

OP. 76 NO. 6 IN E FLAT
Movement II   bb. 1-39   pp. 78-9

OP. 77 NO. 2 IN F
Movement II   bb. 1-78   pp. 92-3
                  bb. 79-127   pp. 95-6

About the Authors
& Performers

ALAN GEORGE is a founder member of the Fitzwilliam String Quartet, with whom he has played all over Europe, North America and Japan. Included among their many recordings for Decca is the first-ever complete set of the fifteen quartets of Shostakovich (who befriended them near the end of his life). Since 1976, he has also been actively involved in the period-instrument movement and has been principal viola in the Orchestre Révolutionnaire et Romantique. He is the author of three studies of Shostakovich's chamber music, and now divides his time between the Fitzwilliam and his classes in viola and chamber music at the RNCM. Together with his wife Lesley, he runs a registered charity – Jessie's Fund, a memorial to their nine-year-old daughter – which is committed to helping sick children through the therapeutic use of music.

JOHN IRVING is Senior Lecturer in Music at the University of Bristol, where he has taught since 1988. Previously he held lectureships at New College, Oxford and Birmingham University, and was Ida Carroll Research Fellow at the RNCM between 1984 and 1986. His published research focuses on two main areas: English renaissance instrumental music and Mozart, and includes the *Musica Britannica* edition of *Tomkins's Consort Music* (Stainer and Bell, 1991); *The Anders von Dueben Keyboard Tablature* (American Institute of Musicology/Hänssler Verlag, 2000); *Mozart's Piano Sonatas: Contexts, Source, Style* (Cambridge University Press, 1997); and *Mozart: The 'Haydn' Quartets* (Cambridge University Press, 1998). He is a contributor to the forthcoming *Mozart: Composer Companion* (Oxford University Press) and *The Cambridge History of Nineteenth Century Music* (Cambridge University Press).

DENIS McCALDIN is a musicologist and a conductor. He is Director of the Haydn Society of Great Britain and Professor of Performance Studies at Lancaster University. His research interests are centred on Haydn and on choral and instrumental music of the eighteenth and twentieth centuries. His list of publications

features scholarly editions of a number of Haydn's works in-
cluding his *Te Deum*, *F major Mass*, *Little Organ Mass*, and *Nelson
Mass* (OUP and Faber), studies of Mahler and Stravinsky
(Novello), and Beethoven's choral music (published by Faber in
The Beethoven Companion). He has worked with many major
British orchestras, and in Australia, Africa, Europe and North
America. Through his association with the UK's and Europe's
foremost chamber orchestras, he has developed a special interest
in the chamber orchestra repertoire, commissioning new works
and rediscovering forgotten ones.

H. C. ROBBINS LANDON is the world's leading authority on the
life and music of Haydn; his five-volume *Haydn: Chronicle and
Works* (1976-80) is the definitive study of the composer. As a
writer and editor, Robbins Landon's output is vast, and includes
works not only on Haydn, but also Mozart, Beethoven, Gluck
and other composers of the Classical era. Research interests in
the music of the Baroque are reflected in writings on Handel and
on the glories of Venice. H. C. Robbins Landon is also a well-
known broadcaster and lecturer on a wide range of musical topics.

MICHAEL SPITZER lectures in music at Durham University. He
has published articles on Haydn, Beethoven and aspects of music
theory including semiotics. He is currently completing a book
on music and metaphor.

DAVID WYN JONES is Senior Lecturer in Music at Cardiff Univer-
sity. He has written extensively on music of the Classical period.
His books include *Haydn: His Life and Music* (co-authored with
H. C. Robbins Landon), a study of Beethoven's Pastoral Sym-
phony in the 'Cambridge Handbook' series, and a biography of
Beethoven in the 'Musical Lives' series. He is also the editor of
Music in eighteenth-century Austria and *Music in eighteenth-century
Britain*. At present he is compiling a major new reference vol-
ume on Haydn, the *Oxford Companion to Haydn*, due for publi-
cation in 2001. For Chandos he is acting as an advisor for the
complete recording of Haydn's masses performed by CM90 and
Richard Hickox.

DAVID YOUNG's research and teaching interests centre on the music of the Classical era, with particular reference to Haydn, Mozart and Beethoven. His writings have appeared in several journals, including the *Research Chronicle* as well as the new edition of *The New Grove Dictionary of Music and Musicians*. David Young is Academic Registrar at the Royal Northern College of Music.

THE YEOMANS STRING QUARTET
     Robert Yeomans *violin* Anne Bünemann *violin* Louise
     Lansdown *viola* Gabriel Waite *cello*
The Yeomans String Quartet was formed in September 1998 at the Royal Northern College of Music. In 1999, the quartet played at the HaydnFest, and was awarded a scholarship to attend a chamber music course under Michael Bochmann in Cheltenham. The quartet went on to perform at Dunham Massey National Trust, at the RNCM, in Northern Germany in June and in South Africa in December. The year 2000 began with a recital in the QuartetFest held at the RNCM, followed by recitals in Cheltenham, Machynlleth in North Wales, Warwickshire Summer Chamber Music Series, Lady Lever Art Gallery in Liverpool, and Buxton Music Festival; the quartet also participated in the twenty-fourth Academy of String Quartets held at the Britten-Pears School in Snape, and made a concert tour to north-eastern Italy. The quartet has received coaching from Christopher Rowland, Alan George, Shmuel Ashkenazy, Roger Bigley, Vicci Wardman, Michael Bochmann, Hugh MacGuire, Milan Skampa and Stefan Metz. The Yeomans String Quartet has been invited to perform with Northwest Classical Music Tours in 2001.

Select Bibliography

Auer, Leopold, *Violin Playing As I Teach It* (New York: Frederick A. Stokes, 1921)

Bartha, D. (ed.), *Joseph Haydn Gesammelte Briefe und Aufzeichnungen: Unter Benützung der Quellensammlung von H. C. Robbins Landon* (Kassel: Bärenreiter, 1965)

Dalhouse, Carl, *Foundations of Music History*, translated by J. Bradford Robinson (Cambridge: Cambridge University Press, 1983)

Drabkin, William, 'Beethoven and the Open String', *Music Analysis* 4 (1985)

---'The Cello Part in Beethoven's Late Quartets', *Beethoven Forum* 7 (1999)

---'Fingering in Haydn's Quartets', *Early Music* 16 (1988)

---*A Reader's Guide to Haydn's Early String Quartets* (Westport, Connecticut: Greenwood Press, 2000)

Feder, Georg, 'Ein vergessener Haydn-Brief', *Haydn-Studien* I/2 (1966)

Gotwals, V. (ed.), *Haydn: Two Contemporary Portraits* (Wisconsin: University of Wisconsin Press, 1963)

Griesinger, Georg August, 'Biographische Notizen über Joseph Haydn', serialised in *Allgemeine musikalische Zeitung* xi (1809), and issued in Leipzig the following year as a single work. Translated in H.C. Robbins Landon, *Haydn: Chronicle and Works. The Early Years* (London: Thames & Hudson, 1976)

Hertz, Daniel, *Haydn, Mozart and the Viennese School* (New York and London: Norton, 1995)

Hoboken, Anthony van, *Joseph Haydn: Thematisch-Bibliographisches Werkverzeichnis*, Band I (Mainz: Schott, 1957)

Hosler, Bellamy, *Changing Aesthetic Views of Instrumental Music in Eighteenth-Century Germany* (Ann Arbor: UMI Press, 1981)

Hunter, Mary, 'Haydn's London Piano Trios and His Salomon String Quartets: Private vs. Public?', in *Haydn and His World*, ed. Elaine Sisman (Princeton: Princeton University Press, 1997)

Hughes, Rosemary, *Haydn String Quartets* (London: BBC, 1966)

Landon, H. C. Robbins, *Haydn: Chronicle and Works. Haydn in England* (London: Thames & Hudson, 1976)

---*Haydn: Chronicle and Works. Haydn at Eszterháza 1766-1790* (London: Thames & Hudson, 1978)

---*Haydn: Chronicle and Works. The Early Years* (London: Thames

& Hudson, 1980)

---and Mitchell, Donald, (eds.), 'The Chamber Music' in *The Mozart Companion* (London: Faber, 1956)

Morrow, Mary S., *German Music Criticism in the Late Eighteenth Century* (Cambridge: Cambridge University Press, 1997)

Mozart, Leopold, *Versuch einer gründlichen Violinschule* (Augsburg, 1756), translated by Editha Knocker as *A Treatise on the Fundamental Principles of Playing the Violin*, 2nd edition (London: Oxford University Press, 1967)

Neubauer, John *The Emancipation of Music from Language: Departure from Mimesis in Eighteenth-Century Aesthetics* (New Haven: Yale University Press, 1986)

Pohl, Carl Ferdinand, *Joseph Haydn*, iii (Leipzig: Hugo Bostiber, 1927)

Ratner, Leonard G., *Classic Music: Expression, Form, and Style* (New York: Schirmer Books, 1980)

Rosen, Charles, *The Classical Style* (London: Faber & Faber, 1971)

Scholes, Percy (ed.), *Dr. Burney's Musical Tours in Europe*, Vol. II (Central Europe and the Netherlands, 1773 and 1775) (London: Oxford University Press, 1959)

Schroeder, David, *Haydn and the Enlightenment: the Late Symphonies and their Audience* (Oxford: Clarendon Press, 1990)

Somfai, László, 'A Bold Enharmonic Modulatory Model in Joseph Haydn's String Quartets', in *Studies in Eighteenth-Century Music*, ed. H.C. Robbins Landon (London: Allen and Unwin, 1970)

---'Haydn's London String Quartets', in *Haydn Studies: Proceedings of the International Haydn Conference, Washington D.C. 1975*, ed. Jens Peter Larsen, Howard Serwer and James Webster (New York: Norton, 1981)

Spitzer, Michael, 'The Retransition as Sign: Listener-Orientated Approaches to Tonal Closure in Haydn's Sonata-Form Movements', *Journal of the RMA* 121 (1996)

Sutcliffe, W. Dean, *Haydn String Quartets, op. 50* (Cambridge: Cambridge University Press, 1992)

Tovey, Donald Francis, 'Haydn', in *Cobbett's Cyclopedic Survey of Chamber Music*, Vol. I (London: Oxford University Press, 1929)

Webster, James, 'Sonata Form' in *The New Grove Dictionary of Music and Musicians* (London: Macmillan, 1980)

---*Haydn's Farewell Symphony and the Idea of Classical Style: Through-Composition and Cyclic Integration in his Instrumental Music* (Cambridge: Cambridge University Press, 1991)

Index

Abert 9
Albrechtsberger 11, 35
Amsterdam 15
Apponyi, Count 12, 51
Artaria 15, 16, 17, 18, 43, 85, 124
Articulation [in performance] 127-131
Auer, Leopold 127

Bach, J.S. 33, 129
Barrett Ayres, Reginald 8, 124
Bartoli, Cecilia 10
Bartók 71
Batteux, Charles 19
Beethoven 9, 10, 55, 58, 99, 120,
121, 122, 133, 134
[Opera] *Fidelio* 60
Piano Concertos
Second 62
Fourth 66
Piano Sonatas
op. 2 93
'Hammerklavier' 106, 120
'Waldstein' 62
String Quartets
op. 18 93, 122
18/1 134
18/3 62
18/6 58, 120
op. 59 131
59/1 53
op. 95 [in F sharp minor] 123
op. 109 120
op. 111 120
op. 127 [in C minor] 120
op. 130 [in B flat] 106
op. 131 [in C sharp minor] 120
op. 135 [in F] 99
op. 133 Grosse Fuge 120, 123, 129
String Trios
op. 9 93
Symphonies
Third [C minor] 117
Fifth Symphony 133
Sixth Symphony 133
Seventh Symphony 62, 133
Eighth Symphony 57
Ninth Symphony 66, 78, 130

Berlin 15
Blume, Friedrich 39
Boileau, Nicolas 19
Bows [instrument] 124-127
'transitional' 125
'Baroque' 125
Brahms 121
Breitkopf & Härtel 134
British Library 124
Burney, Charles 18, 63

[CD track references in text]
CD 1 37
CD 2 39
CD 3 44
CD 4 47
CD 5 51
CD 6 64
CD 7 66
CD 8 70
CD 9 71
CD 10 72
CD 11 75
CD 12 78
CD 13 82
CD 14 86
CD 15 87
CD 16 90
CD 17 91
CD 18 102
CD 19 106
CD 20 110
CD 21 113
CD 22 117
Cadiz 46
Cobbett 9
'complementarity' 26, 27, 28
counterpoint 23 ff.
Czerny 34, 133, 134

Dahlhaus, Carl 13, 31
Debussy 121
Dittersdorf 131
Doblinger K.G. 7, 8, 124
Drabkin, William 108, 131
Dvořák 94

Early Music movement   132
Edition Peters   89, 123, 124
Embellishment [in performance]
                            131-3
Empfindsamkeit   13, 27
Enlightenment   110
Erdödy, Count   18, 51, 116
Esterházy [court etc.]   20, 38, 46, 51
Esterházy, Prince Nikolaus   38, 51
Esterházys, the   46
Eszterháza   7
Eulenberg   124

Feder, Georg   16
Fitzwilliam Quartet   126, 135
Forster, William 1   7
Four-movement design [in
    Haydn's quartets]   19
Fürnberg, Baron   11, 13, 35

Gebrauchmusik   18
Gli Scherzi [Haydn's op. 33]   86
'Gott! Erhalte Franz den
    Kaiser' [Emperor's Hymn]   67, 117
Gottsched, Johann Christoph   19
Gotwals, V.   96
Griesinger, Georg August   11, 35
Grove, The New [1980]   34, 35
Gut strings   125, 126, 127

Hanover Square Rooms   51
Harnoncourt, Nikolaus   10
Haydn
    [Cantata] *Scena di Berenice*   10
    [Oratorio] *The Creation*   117, 121
    String Quartets
    op. 1   19, 58, 67, 134
        1/1   11, 33, 35-9, 63, 82-5,
                87, 91, 100, 102-5,
                109, 120, 122, 136
        1/3   58
        1/6   64, 136
    op. 2   19, 58, 67, 122, 134
        2/6   58, 69
    op. 9   14, 19, 25, 28, 38,
                39, 42, 58, 103
        9/1   26, 27, 28, 30, 39, 122
        9/2   65
        9/5   57, 58, 69
    op. 17   14, 38, 39, 42, 58, 122
        17/4   33, 39-42, 44,
        17/5   65

op. 20   14, 15, 23, 38, 42, 43,
                            58, 122
'Sun' quartets [op. 20]   105
op. 20 fugal finales   14, 20, 23, 24
    20/1   57
    20/2   23, 66, 67, 100, 105-
                110, 113, 120, 136
    20/4   69, 70
    20/5   13, 23, 69, 70, 109
    20/6   23, 109
op. 33   14, 16, 23, 43, 46, 58,
                85, 86, 110, 122
    33/1   68
    33/2   33, 43-6, 47, 68, 85-91
    33/3   129
    33/5   100, 110-113, 120
op. 42   14, 46, 57, 58
op. 50   14, 16, 17, 25, 29, 46
    50/1   69, 70, 72
    50/3   21, 69
    50/5   68
    50/6   30, 60, 68
op. 54   14, 46, 119
    54/1   57
    54/2   24, 57, 58, 69, 70, 71,
                100, 113-6, 120, 133
    54/3   69
op. 55   14, 46
    55/2   69, 77, 78
    55/3   69
op. 64   14, 46, 47, 59, 75, 130
    64/1   57, 69
    64/2   60, 69
    64/3   69, 72
    64/4   69, 72
    64/5   20, 33, 46-51, 53,
                        69, 72-4
    64/6   29, 69, 72, 131
op. 71   12, 14, 51, 116, 122,
                        123, 131
    71/1   12, 69
    71/2   12, 69, 133
    71/3   12, 69
op. 74   12, 14, 51, 60, 61, 116
    74/1   118
    74/2   69
    74/3   12, 60, 69, 75-6, 131
op. 76   14, 18, 51, 60, 61,
                101, 110, 116, 119,
                        122, 130
    76/1   69, 93, 117
    76/2   20, 52, 69, 117

76/3   18, 67, 69, 100,116-120
76/4   20, 33, 51-6
76/5   9, 60, 61, 68
76/6   61, 78-9, 136
op. 77   14, 25, 51, 122, 130, 134
77/1   22, 25, 93, 130, 134
77/2   24, 25, 58, 69, 91-96,
                 133, 134, 135
op. 103   14, 25, 60, 69, 94, 99
Seven Last Words 46, 57, 124, 134
String quartets, Slow Movements in
  keys of   59-62
  position of   59
  quartets with two   58
  a third from tonic   61
  variation form in   69
Symphonies
  'Paris'   17
  'London'   130, 133
  no. 7   65
  no. 45   60
  no. 70   77
  no. 99   60
HaydnFest   7, 8, 136
Henle   124
Hensel, Fanny   9
Hertz, Daniel   63
Hoboken, Anthony van   15
Hughes, Rosemary   39, 54
Hummel   133
Hunter, Mary   12

Instruments   124-127
  Period   125
  Classical   126

Kalmus, Alfred A., Ltd   8
Keller, Hans   21, 46, 47, 53

Landon, H.C. Robbins   8, 11, 16,
           19, 21, 35, 62, 84, 124
Larsen, Jens Peter   12
Lavater, Johann Caspar   16, 43
Lobkowitz, Prince   25
London   15, 51
Longman and Broderip   17

Mälzel, Johann Nepomuk   133
Mahler   121
Mendelssohn, Felix   9, 10
Meng, Anton Raphael   66

Mitchell, Donald   21
monothematicism   24, 25, 39, 46, 52
mordents   132
Morrow, Mary Sue   19
Moscheles, Felix   9
Mozart, Leopold   127, 129, 132, 133
                          134
Mozart, W. A.   9, 50, 60, 120,121,
                       122, 131
  Chamber Music
  String quartets   121
    Quartet K. 170   63
    G minor String Quintet 113
  Operas
    Cosè fan tutte,   9, 60
    Zauberflöte   60
  Symphonies
    no. 39 K. 543   87
    'Haffner'   130

'new and special way', a   43, 44, 44,
                        85, 110
Notation   127-131

Ornamentation [in performance]
                        131-3
Öttingen-Wallerstein, Fürsten
  Kraft Ernst zu   16

Paris   15
parody   26, 27, 28, 101
Peters Edition   89, 123, 124
Pohl, Carl Ferdinand   9

Ratner, Leonard G.   62, 74
Repertoire, concept of   14
Rosen, Charles   33, 34, 42

Salomon, Johann Peter   12, 51, 123
Schlecht, Abbot Robert,
  of Salmannsweiler (Baden)   16
Scholes, Percy   63
Schroeder, David   43, 44, 46
Schubert   121
  G major Quartet op. 161   77
Serwer, Howard   12
Shostakovich   130
Sisman, Elaine   12
slur signs [in performance] 128
Smetana   121
Somfai, László   12, 62, 80

sonata form   130
sonata principle   33 ff.
Sutcliffe, W. Dean   17, 28, 29, 43, 46

Tchaikovsky   122
tempo [in performance]   133-5
'topics'   62-7
Tost, Johann   7, 20, 46, 47, 51, 77
Tovey, Donald Francis   63
trills [in performance]   132

Vanhal   131
Versuch einer gründlichen Violinschule
   [Leopold Mozart]   127
vibrato   127
Vienna   15, 35, 51
(Gesellschaft der Musikfreunde)
                                   124

Webster, James   12, 34, 100, 110
Weinzierl   35

Yeomans String Quartet   7